crochet
for
Barbie®
doll

crochet

for

Barbie®

doll

75 delightful creations to crochet

by

Nicky Epstein

SOHO PUBLISHING COMPANY
NEW YORK

SOHO PUBLISHING COMPANY
233 Spring Street
New York, New York 10013

EDITOR-IN-CHIEF
Trisha Malcolm

ART DIRECTOR
Chi Ling Moy

BOOK MANAGER
Theresa McKeon

CONTRIBUTING EDITOR
Michelle Lo

INSTRUCTIONS EDITORS
Pat Harste
Carla Scott

INSTRUCTIONS PROOFREADER
Emily Harste

YARN EDITOR
Veronica Manno

PHOTOGRAPHY
Bobb Connors
Jack Deutsch

STYLISTS
Christina Batch
Rebecca Rosen
Lisa Ventry

PRODUCTION MANAGERS
Lillian Esposito
David Joinnides

PRESIDENT, SOHO PUBLISHING COMPANY
Art Joinnides

Library of Congress Cataloging-in-Publication Data

Crochet for Barbie Doll: 75 delightful creations to crochet / [Nicky Epstein].
    p. cm.
    ISBN 1-931543-06-2
    1. Crocheting. 2. Barbie dolls. I. Title

TT820.E67 2002
746.43'4043–dc21   2001049632

Manufactured in China

1 3 5 7 9 10 8 6 4 2

First Edition

I'll never forget the day in 1959 my parents bought me the original Barbie® doll. I fell in love with her, and with my mother's and grandmother's help, I began knitting and crocheting for my new doll.

Who knew that more than forty years later Barbie would still be the world's favorite fashion doll and that I would have an opportunity to create a knitting book for her, "Knits for Barbie® Doll"?

The success of that book is a testament to the public's long love affair with Barbie. I was so gratified to see how it not only got adults excited about knitting for Barbie but also encouraged children who wanted to learn how to knit.

Everyone was happy. Everyone, that is, except those who prefer crocheting to knitting and wished they had a Barbie book of their own. Their wish became my inspiration for creating this "Crochet for Barbie® Doll" book.

Creating all-new designs for this book was as challenging as it was fun. I've included everything from casual wear to haute couture, colorful little hats to fashionable ensembles. You'll also find outfits and accessories for Barbie and her friends, including Ken.

I've made sure to include designs that accommodate all levels of crocheting skills with the hope that they will enhance your Barbie® doll's wardrobe.

"Crochet for Barbie Doll" was a labor of love for me, and I hope you will enjoy working on these pieces as much as I enjoyed designing them. I truly believe that Barbie and her fans will take pleasure in their new "hand-crocheted" heirlooms, which they can pass down to the next Barbie generation with pride.

Happy crocheting for your Barbie doll,

Nicky Epstein

To my brother Benjamin, who tore the head off my first Barbie (accidentally), and to Tyson, Scott and Tristan, whom I love so much.

Table of Contents

Perky Plaid

This smart ensemble takes Barbie® to the office in classic style. Transform a basic pullover into a stylish wardrobe "essential" by adding three-quarter length sleeves, a mock turtleneck and ribbed edging. It works wonderfully with the windowpane plaid skirt, featuring dramatic color contrast.

skirt

Made in one piece. Beg at bottom edge with larger hook and A, ch 41.
Row 1 (RS): With A, sc in 2nd ch from hook and in next 4 ch, [with B, sc in next ch, with A, sc in next 4 ch] twice, with B, sc in next ch, with A, sc in next 8 ch, [with B, sc in next ch, with A, sc in next 4 ch] twice, with B, sc in next ch, with A, sc in last 5 ch—40 sts. Ch 1, turn. **Rows 2-8:** With A, sc in first 5 sts, [with B, sc in next st, with A, sc in next 4 sts] twice, with B, sc in next st, with A, sc in next 8 sts, [with B, sc in next st, with A, sc in next 4 sts] twice, with B, sc in next st, with A, sc in last 5 sts. Ch 1, turn. After row 8 is completed, join B, ch 1, turn. **Row 9 (RS):** With B, sc in each st across. Join A, ch 1, turn. **Rows 10-16:** Rep row 2. After row 16 is completed, join B, ch 1, turn. **Row 17:** Rep row 9. Join A, ch 1, turn. Rep row 2 until piece measures 2⅝" from beg, end on WS.

Shape Waist
Dec Row 1: Keeping to color pat as established, sc in first 2 sts, dec 1 st over next 2 sts, [sc in next 3 sts, dec 1 st over next 2 sts] 3 times, sc in next 2 sts, dec 1 st over next 2 sts, [sc in next 3 sts, dec 1 st over next 2 sts] 3 times, sc in last 2 sts—32 sts. **Following Row:** Work even in pat st as established. **Dec Row 2:** With A only, sc across dec 4 sts evenly spaced—28 sts. **Following Row:** With A only, sc in each st across. Fasten off.

FINISHING
Lightly steam-press skirt. Sew back seam to within 1" of top edge. Sew a snap to waist opening.

pullover

BACK
Ribbing: Ribbing is made vertically. With smaller hook and B, ch 5. **Row 1:** Sc in 2nd ch from hook and in each ch across—4 sts. Ch 1, turn. **Row 2:** Working through back lps only, sc in each st across. Ch 1, turn. Rep row 2 for rib pat and work even until piece measures 2½" from beg. Ch 1, turn to long edge of ribbing. **Row 1 (RS):** Work 24 sc evenly spaced across long edge of ribbing. Change to larger hook, ch 1, turn. **Row 2:** Sc in each st across. Ch 1, turn. Rep row 2 for pat st and work even until piece measures 2" from beg, end on WS. Do not ch, turn.
Armholes
Sl st across first 3 sts, ch 1, sc across to within last 3 sts—18 sts. Ch 1, turn. Work even until piece measures 2½" from beg, end on WS.
Divide for Back Opening
First Side: Work across first 9 sts, ch 1, turn. Work even until piece measures 3½" from beg. Fasten off.
Second Side: From RS, join B in next st with a sc. Work across last 8 sts—9

sts. Ch 1, turn. Work same as for right half to shoulder. Fasten off.

FRONT
Work same as for back, omitting back opening, until piece measures 2¾" from beg.
Shape Neck
First Side—Next Row: Sc across first 7 sts. Ch 1, turn. Dec 1 st at neck edge on next row, then every row once more—5 sts. Work even until front measures same length as back to shoulders. Fasten off. **Second Side—Next Row:** Sk 4 center sts, join yarn with a sc in next st, ch 1 work across last 6 sts—7 sts. Ch 1, turn. Continue to work same as first side. Fasten off.

SLEEVES
Ribbing: With smaller hook and B, ch 4. **Row 1:** Sc in 2nd ch from hook and in each ch across—3 sts. Ch 1, turn. **Row 2:** Working through back lps only, sc in each st across. Ch 1, turn. Rep row 2 for rib pat and work even until piece measures 1¼" from beg. Ch 1, turn to long edge of ribbing. **Row 1 (RS):** Work 16 sc evenly spaced across long edge of ribbing. Change to larger hook, ch 1, turn. **Row 2:** Sc in each st across. Ch 1, turn. Working in sc, inc 1 st each side on next row, then every 4th row once more—20 sts. Work even until sleeve measures 1½" from beg. Fasten off.

FINISHING
Lightly steam-press all pieces; do not press ribbings.
Mock Turtleneck
With smaller hook and B, ch 5. Work in ribbing same as for back until piece measures 3¾" from beg. Fasten off. Sew shoulder seams. Sew mock turtleneck to neck edge. Sew on sleeves. Sew side and sleeve seams. Sew 1 snap to mock turtleneck.

materials

Yarn
True 4ply Botany (50g/170m) by Rowan, 1 ball each #546 Jet (A) and #585 Grape (B).
Crochet Hooks
Sizes B (1) and C (2) or size to obtain gauge.
Notions
Tapestry needle.
2 small metal snaps.

notes

1. When changing colors, draw new color through 2 lps on hook to complete sc.
2. Do not carry color B across, instead use a separate 36"-long strand of B for each vertical stripe on skirt.

gauge

15 sc and 18 rows = 2" (using larger hook).
FOR PROPER FIT, TAKE THE TIME TO CHECK YOUR GAUGE.

Style Setter

"fur"-trimmed cardigan

Fabulous "fur"-trimmed collar and cuffs, crystal bead closure, and delicate eyelet stitches work together to create this chic cardigan.

BACK

Beg at bottom edge, with MC, ch 26. **Foundation Row (WS):** Sc in 2nd ch from hook and in each ch across—25 sts. Ch 1, turn. **Following Row:** Sc in each st across. Ch 1, turn.

Pattern Stitch

Row 1 (WS): Sc in first st, * ch 1, sk next st, sc in next st, rep from * across. Ch 1, turn. **Row 2 (RS):** Sc in first st, * sc over next ch-1 sp, sc in next sc, rep from * across. Ch 1, turn. Rep rows 1 and 2 until piece measures 2" from beg, end on WS. Do not ch, turn.

Armholes

Sl st in first st, then over ch-1 sp and next sc, ch 1, work across to within last 3 sts (2 sc and 1 ch-1 sp)—19 sts. Ch 1, turn. Establish pat st as follows—**Row 3:** Sc in first 2 sts, * ch 1, sk next st, sc in next st, rep from * across, end sc in last st. Ch 1, turn. **Row 4:** Sc in first 2 sts, * sc over next ch-1 sp, sc in next sc, rep from * across, end sc in last st. Ch 1, turn. Rep rows 3 and 4 until piece measures 3½" from beg, end on RS. Fasten off.

Yarn
Richesse et Soie (25g/approx 145yd) by K1C2, 1 ball #9918 Fog (MC) and Fuzzy Stuff (20yd) by Rainbow Gallery, 1 card #FZ02 Black (CC).
Crochet Hook
Size C (2) or size to obtain gauge.
Notions
Tapestry needle.
5 (3mm) Crystal Round Beads #13012 from Mill Hill.

notes

1. When changing colors, draw new color through 2 lps on hook to complete sc.
2. It's sometimes difficult seeing the sts when working with fuzzy yarn. For best results, count sts as you work across each row to make sure you do not skip or miss a st.

gauge

6 sc = 1" (using MC).
FOR PROPER FIT, TAKE THE TIME TO CHECK YOUR GAUGE.

Style Setter

Pair the cardigan with slacks or a long, slim skirt. Crochets up quickly in cashmere/silk blend and fuzzy yarns.

LEFT FRONT

Beg at bottom edge, with MC, ch 16. **Foundation Row (WS):** Sc in 2nd ch from hook and in each ch across—15 sts. Ch 1, turn.

Following Row: Sc in each st across. Ch 1, turn.

Pattern Stitch and Front Band

Row 1 (WS): Sc in first 3 sts, * ch 1, sk next st, sc in next st, rep from * across. Ch 1, turn. **Row 2 (RS):** Sc in first st, * sc over next ch-1 sp, sc in next sc, rep from * across, end sc in last 2 sts. Ch 1, turn. Rep rows 1 and 2 until piece measures 2" from beg, end on WS. Do not ch, turn.

Armhole

Sl st in first st, then over ch-1 sp and next sc, ch 1, finish row—12 sts. Ch 1, turn. Establish pat st as follows—**Row 3:** Sc in first 3 sts, * ch 1, sk next st, sc in next st, rep from * across, end sc in last st. Ch 1, turn. **Row 4:** Sc in first 2 sts, * sc over next ch-1 sp, sc in next sc, rep from * across, end sc in last 2 sts. Ch 1, turn. Rep rows 3 and 4 until piece measures 3" from beg, end on WS.

Shape Neck

Keeping to pat st, work across first 7 sts, ch 1, turn. Dec 1 st at neck edge on next row, then every row once more—5 sts. Work even until piece measures same length as back to shoulders. Fasten off.

RIGHT FRONT

Beg at bottom edge, with MC, ch 16. **Foundation Row (WS):** Sc in 2nd ch from hook and in each ch across—15 sts. Ch 1, turn.

Following Row: Sc in each st across. Ch 1, turn.

Pattern Stitch and Front Band

Row 1 (WS): Sc in first st, * ch 1, sk next st, sc in next st, rep from * across, end sc in last 2 sts. Ch 1, turn. **Row 2 (RS):** Sc in first 3 sts, * sc over next ch-1 sp, sc in next sc, rep from * across. Ch 1, turn. Rep rows 1 and 2 until piece measures 2" from beg, end on WS. Ch1, turn.

Armhole

Work across to within last 3 sts (2 sc and 1 ch-1 sp)—12 sts. Ch 1, turn. Establish pat st as follows—**Row 3:** Sc in first 2 sts, * ch 1, sk next st, sc in next st, rep from * across, end sc in last 2 sts. Ch 1, turn. **Row 4:** Sc in first 3 sts, * sc over next ch-1 sp, sc in next sc, rep from * across, end sc in last st. Ch 1, turn. Rep rows 3 and 4 until piece measures 3" from beg, end on WS. Do not ch, turn.

Shape Neck

Sl st across first 5 sts, ch 1, finish row. Ch 1, turn. Dec 1 st at neck edge on next row, then every row once more—5 sts. Work even until piece measures same length as back to shoulders. Fasten off.

SLEEVES

Sew shoulder seams. From RS, with MC work 23 sts evenly spaced along armhole edge. Ch 1, turn. Rep pat st rows 1 and 2 same as for back until sleeve measures 1" from beg, end on WS. Keeping to pat st, dec 1 st each side on next row, then every 4th row 3 times more—15 sts. Work even until sleeve measures 3" from beg, end on RS. Join CC, ch 1, turn.

Fur Cuff

Work even in sc for 4 rows. Fasten off.

FINISHING

Fur Collar

From RS, sk first 3 sts of right neck shaping, join CC with a sc in next st, work 19 more sts evenly spaced to within last 3 sts of left neck shaping—20 sts. Ch 1, turn. Work even until collar measures ³⁄₄" from beg. Fasten off.

Sew side and sleeve seams. Turn up fur cuffs. On left front, sew 1 bead just below beg of neck shaping, then another ¹⁄₄" from bottom edge. Sew 3 more beads spaced evenly between. To close cardigan, push beads between sts.

Height of Luxury

From Scandinavia and Canada to the UK and Japan, Barbie® always looks great. This snazzy coat features a "fur"-trimmed hood and cuffs in soft angora; perfect for chasing away the chills. A modified moss-stitch is used for the coat and matching scarf, offering attractive textural dimension.

coat

BACK
With smaller hook and MC, ch 33. **Row 1 (WS):** Sc in 2nd ch from hook, * hdc in next ch, sc in next ch, rep from * across, end hdc in last ch—32 sts. Ch 1, turn. **Row 2:** * Sc in next st, hdc in next st, rep from * across. Ch 1, turn. Rep row 2 for pat st and work even until piece measures 1½" from beg, end on WS.

Shape Sides
Dec 1 st each side on next row, then every 1" 3 times more—24 sts, AT THE SAME TIME, keep to pat st as follows: always work a sc over a hdc and a hdc over a sc. When you end with a sc, ch 2 to turn. When you end with a hdc, ch 1 to turn. Work even until piece measures 8" from beg, end on WS. Fasten off.

LEFT FRONT
With smaller hook and MC, ch 21. **Row 1 (WS):** Sc in 2nd ch from hook, * hdc in next ch, sc in next ch, rep from * across, end hdc in last ch—20 sts. Ch 1, turn. **Row 2:** * Sc in

next st, hdc in next st, rep from * across. Ch 1, turn. Rep row 2 for pat st and work even until piece measures 1½" from beg, end on WS.

Shape Side
Keeping to pat st, dec 1 st at beg of next row, then at same edge every 1" 3 times more—16 sts. Work even until piece measures 7½" from beg, end on WS.

Shape Neck
Next Row: Work across first 9 sts, ch 2, turn. Keeping to pat st, dec 1 st at neck edge every row 3 times—6 sts. Fasten off.

RIGHT FRONT
Work same as for left front to neck shaping, reversing side shaping, end on WS. Do not ch, turn.

Shape Neck
Next Row: Sl st across first 9 sts, ch 1, finish row. Keeping to pat st, dec 1 st at neck edge every row 3 times—6 sts. Fasten off.

SLEEVES
Sew shoulder seams. From RS, measure and mark 1½" down from each shoulder seam on fronts and back. From RS with smaller hook and MC, join yarn with a sc at marker. Work 23 more sc evenly spaced across armhole edge to next marker—24 sts. Ch 1, turn. **Row 2:** * Sc in next st, hdc in next st, rep from * across. Ch 1, turn. Rep row 2 for pat st and work even until sleeve measures 1" from beg, end on WS. Keeping to pat st, dec 1 st each side on next row, then every ½" once more—20 sts. Work even until sleeve measures 2" from beg, end on WS.

Fur Cuffs
Join CC. Change to larger hook, ch 1, turn. **Next Row:** Sc in first st, * sk next st, sc in next st, rep from *

across, end sc in last st—11 sts. Ch 1, turn. Work even in sc for 2 more rows. Fasten off.

FINISHING
Sew side and sleeve seams.
Hood
From RS with smaller hook and MC, join yarn with a sc after last sl st of right front neck shaping. Work 23 more sc evenly spaced across neck edge to left neck shaping—24 sts. Ch 1, turn. **Row 2:** * Sc in next st, hdc in next st, rep from * across. Ch 1, turn. Rep row 2 for pat st and work even until hood measures 3" from beg, end on WS. Fasten off. Sew hood seam.

"Fur" Trim
From RS with larger hook and CC, join yarn with a sc in first row of hood on right front. Work 31 more sc evenly spaced across front edge of hood—32 sts. Ch 1, turn. Work even in sc for 2 more rows. Fasten off. Sew side edges of "fur" trim to neck edge.
On left front, sew first pearl button ¼" from top neck edge and ¼" from front edge. Sew last button 2¾" from top neck edge and ¼" from front edge. Sew 2 remaining buttons, centered between them. To close coat, push beads between sts.

scarf
Scarf is made vertically. Beg at long side edge with smaller hook and MC, ch 97. **Row 1:** Sc in 2nd ch from hook, * hdc in next ch, sc in next ch, rep from * across, end hdc in last ch—96 sts. Ch 1, turn. **Row 2:** * Sc in next st, hdc in next st, rep from * across. Ch 1, turn. Rep row 2 for pat st and work even until piece measures ¾" from beg. Fasten off.

materials

Yarn
Richesse et Soie (25g/approx 145yd) by K1C2, 2 balls #9249 Garnet (MC) and Rainbow Angora (7yd/6.4m) by Rainbow Gallery, 2 cards #RA18 Black (CC).
Crochet Hooks
Size C (2) and D (3) or size to obtain gauge.
Notions
Tapestry needle.
Large-eye sewing needle.
4 (4mm) gold pearls.

note
When changing colors, draw new color through 2 lps on hook to complete sc.

gauge
8 sts and 7 rows = 1" (in pat st using smaller hook and MC).
FOR PROPER FIT, TAKE THE TIME TO CHECK YOUR GAUGE.

Vive La France

C'est la vie...Barbie® takes Paris by storm wearing a bold black and white striped outfit. Work in single crochet throughout. Make the fun "fur" top using "Fuzzy Stuff" and the coordinating skirt and beret using size 5 pearl cotton. The perfect look for any season.

top

Made in one piece. Beg at bottom edge with larger hook and A, ch 43. **Row 1 (RS):** Sc in 2nd ch from hook and in each ch across—42 sts. Ch 1, turn. **Rows 2–4:** Sc in each st across. Ch 1, turn. After row 4 is completed, join B, ch 1, turn. **Rows 5–8:** Rep row 2. After row 8 is completed, join A, ch 1, turn. **Rows 9–12:** Rep row 2. After row 12 is completed, join B, ch 1, turn. **Rows 13–16:** Rep row 2. After row 16 is completed, join A, ch 1, turn.

Left Back

Next Row (RS): Sc across first 8 sts. Ch 1, turn. **Following Row:** Dec 1 st at beg of row—7 sts. Work even for 2 more rows. Join B and work even for 4 rows. Fasten off.

16

Front

Next Row (RS): Sk next 4 sts (underarm), join A with a sc in next st, sc across next 17 sts—18 sts. Ch 1, turn. **Following Row:** Dec 1 st each side—16 sts. Work even for 2 more rows. Join B, ch 1, turn.

Left Front Neck

Next Row (RS): Sc across first 5 sts. Ch 1, turn. **Following Row:** Dec 1 st at beg of next row—4 sts. Work even for 2 more rows. Fasten off.

Right Front Neck

Next Row (RS): Sk next 6 sts (neck edge), join B with a sc in next st, finish row—5 sts. **Following Row:** Dec 1 st at end of row—4 sts. Work even for 2 more rows. Fasten off.

Right Back

Next Row (RS): Sk next 4 sts (underarm), join A with a sc in next st, sc across last 7 sts—8 sts. Ch 1, turn. **Following Row:** Dec 1 st at end of row—7 sts. Work even for 2 more rows. Join B, ch 1, turn. Work even for 4 rows. Fasten off.

FINISHING

Draw in all loose ends. Sew shoulder seams. Beg at bottom edge, sew back seam to within 1" of top edge. Sew a snap to top back opening.

skirt

Made in one piece. Beg at bottom edge with smaller hook and C, ch 45. **Row 1 (RS):** Sc in 2nd ch from hook and in each ch across—44 sts. Ch 1, turn. **Row 2:** Sc in each st across. Join D, ch 1, turn. Rep row 2 for pat st and work in a stripe pat of 2 rows D and 2 rows C. Work even until piece measures 2¼" from beg, end on RS D row.

Shape Waist

Dec Row 1 (WS): Sc in first 4 sts, [dec 1 st over next 2 sts, sc in next 3 sts] 8 times—36 sts. Join C, ch 1, turn. **Following Row:** Sc in each st across. Ch 1, turn. **Dec Row 2 (WS):** Sc in first 2 sts, [dec 1 st over next 2 sts, sc in next 3 sts] 6 times, dec 1 st over next 2 sts, sc in last 2 sts—29 sts. Join D, ch 1, turn. Work even for 4 rows. Fasten off.

FINISHING

Sew back seam to within 1" of top edge. Sew a snap to waist opening.

beret

With smaller hook and C, ch 3. Join ch with a sl st forming a ring. **Rnd 1:** Work 6 sc over ch. Mark last st made with the safety pin. You will be working in a spiral marking the last st made with the safety pin to indicate end of rnd. **Rnd 2:** Work 2 sc in each st around—12 sts. **Rnd 3:** * Sc in next st, work 2 sc in next st, rep from * around—18 sts. **Rnd 4:** * Sc in next 2 sts, work 2 sc in next st, rep from * around—24 sts; join D when completing last st. **Rnd 5:** * Sc in next 3 sts, work 2 sc in next st, rep from * around—30 sts. **Rnd 6:** * Sc in next 4 sts, work 2 sc in next st, rep from * around—36 sts. **Rnd 7:** * Sc in next 5 sts, work 2 sc in next st, rep from * around—42 sts. **Rnd 8:** * Sc in next 6 sts, work 2 sc in next st, rep from * around—48 sts. **Rnd 9:** * Sc in next 7 sts, work 2 sc in next st, rep from * around—54 sts. **Rnd 10:** * Sc in next 8 sts, work 2 sc in next st, rep from * around—60 sts. **Rnds 11-13:** Work even around. **Rnd 14:** * Sc in next 4 sts, dec 1 st over next 2 sts, rep from * around—50 sts. **Rnd 15:** * Sc in next 3 sts, dec 1 st over next 2 sts, rep from * around—40 sts. **Rnd 16:** * Sc in next 2 sts, dec 1 st over next 2 sts, rep from * around—30 sts. **Rnd 17:** Work even around. Fasten off.

materials

Yarn
Fuzzy Stuff (20yd) by Rainbow Gallery, 2 cards #FZ15 White (A) and 1 card #FZ02 Black (B), and Pearl Cotton #5 (10g/48m) by DMC, 1 ball each Blanc (C) and #310 Black (D).

Crochet Hooks
Size B (1) and C (2) or sizes to obtain gauges.

Notions
Tapestry needle.
2 small metal snaps.
Small safety pin.

notes

1. It's sometimes difficult seeing the sts when working with fuzzy yarn. For best results, count sts as you work across each row to make sure you do not skip or miss a st.
2. When changing colors, draw new color though 2 lps on hook to complete sc.
3. Carry color not in use loosely along side edge of work.

gauges

17 sc and 18 rows = 2" (using larger hook and A or B).
17 sc and 20 rows = 2" (using smaller hook and C or D).
FOR PROPER FIT, TAKE THE TIME TO CHECK YOUR GAUGES.

Bahama Top, Hat and Bag

Barbie® is ready to hit the beach in this Caribbean-inspired ensemble. Sun, sand and surf colors add playful spirit while beaded ties at the neck and back offer functional accents. A sassy sun hat and a roomy beach bag are "shore" essentials for lazy summer days.

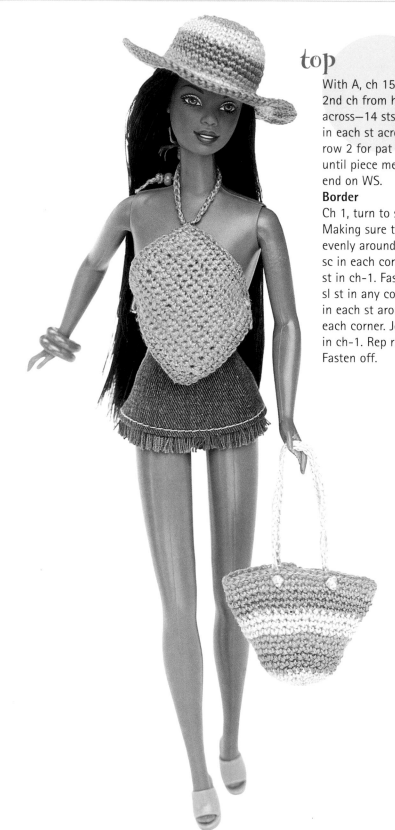

top

With A, ch 15. **Row 1 (WS):** Sc in 2nd ch from hook and in each ch across—14 sts. Ch 1, turn. **Row 2:** Sc in each st across. Ch 1, turn. Rep row 2 for pat st and work even until piece measures 1½" from beg, end on WS.

Border

Ch 1, turn to side edge. **Rnd 1:** Making sure that work lies flat, sc evenly around entire edge, working 3 sc in each corner. Join rnd with a sl st in ch-1. Fasten off. Join C with a sl st in any corner st. **Rnd 2:** Ch 1, sc in each st around, working 3 sc in each corner. Join rnd with a sl st in ch-1. Rep rnd 2 once more. Fasten off.

FINISHING

Draw in all loose ends.

Neck Tie

With C, tightly crochet a ch to measure 5"-long. Fasten off. Sew center of tie to one corner. Thread 1 bead onto each end; knot ends.

Side Ties

(make 2)

Leaving long ends for sewing, with C, tightly crochet a ch to measure 4¼"-long. Fasten off. Sew ties to corners. Thread 1 bead onto each end; knot ends.

hat

With A, ch 3. Join ch with a sl st forming a ring. **Rnd 1:** Work 6 sc over ch. Mark last st made with the safety pin. You will be working in a spiral marking the last st made with the safety pin to indicate end of rnd. **Rnd 2:** Work 2 sc in each st around—12 sts. **Rnd 3:** * Sc in next st, work 2 sc in next st, rep from * around—18 sts. **Rnd 4:** * Sc in next 2 sts, work 2 sc in next st, rep from * around—24 sts. Change to B. **Rnd 5:** * Sc in next 3 sts, work 2 sc in next st, rep from * around—30 sts. **Rnd 6:** * Sc in next 4 sts, work 2 sc in next st, rep from * around—36 sts. **Rnd 7:** Sc in each st around. Change to C. **Rnds 8–10:** Sc in each st around. Change to A. **Rnds 11–13:** Sc in each st around. Change to B.

Brim

Rnd 14: * Sc in next st, work 2 sc in next st, rep from * around—54 sts. **Rnd 15:** Sc in each st around. **Rnd 16:** Rep rnd 14—81 sts. Change to C. **Rnds 17–19:** Sc in each st around. After rnd 19 is completed, join rnd with a sl st in next st. Fasten off.

bag

With B, ch 3. Join ch with a sl st forming a ring. **Rnd 1:** Work 6 sc over ch. Mark last st made with the safety pin. You will be working in a spiral marking the last st made with the safety pin to indicate end of rnd. **Rnd 2:** Work 2 sc in each st around—12 sts. **Rnd 3:** * Sc in next st, work 2 sc in next st, rep from * around—18 sts. **Rnd 4:** * Sc in next 2 sts, work 2 sc in next st, rep from * around—24 sts. Change to C. **Rnds 5 and 6:** Sc in each st around. **Rnd 7:** * Sc in next 3 sts, work 2 sc in next st, rep from * around—30 sts. Change to A. **Rnds 8 and 9:** Sc in each st around. **Rnd 10:** * Sc in next 4 sts, work 2 sc in next st, rep from * around—36 sts. Change to B. **Rnds 11 and 12:** Sc in each st around. **Rnd 13:** * Sc in next 5 sts, work 2 sc in next st, rep from * around—42 sts. Change to C. **Rnds 14 and 15:** Sc in each st around. **Rnd 16:** * Sc in next 6 sts, work 2 sc in next st, rep from * around—48 sts. Change to A. **Rnds 17–19:** Sc in each st around. After rnd 19 is completed, join rnd with a sl st in next st. Fasten off.

FINISHING

Shoulder Straps

(make 2)

Leaving long ends for sewing, with B, tightly crochet a ch to measure 5½"-long. Fasten off. Fold bag flat so color joinings are at center back. For each strap, thread one end into needle. Working from WS to RS, insert needle 2 rows from top edge and ¾" from side edge. Knot end; cut off excess yarn. Rep for each rem end.

materials

Yarn

Rainbow Linen (20yd) by Rainbow Gallery, 1 card each #R414 Terra Cotta (A), #R455 Tan (B) and #R441 Dk. Aqua Green (C).

Crochet Hook

Size B (1) or size to obtain gauge.

Notions

Tapestry needle.
Small safety pin.
4 orange 6/0 "E" beads.

note

When changing colors, draw new color through 2 lps on hook to complete sc.

gauge

9 sc and 10 rnds = 1".
FOR PROPER FIT, TAKE THE TIME TO CHECK YOUR GAUGE.

Sumptuous Luxury

Barbie® is so charming and talented, it's no wonder everybody loves her—she's the life of the party! This gown is fashioned in single crochet using a shimmering metallic yarn. It's styled with a ruched bodice and a sparkling bead accent. The double crochet shrug, made in a novelty "fur" yarn, is the perfect wrap for any evening affair.

gown

Made in one piece. Beg at bottom edge with larger hook and A, ch 43. **Row 1 (WS):** Sc in 2nd ch from hook and in each ch across—42 sts. Ch 1, turn. **Row 2:** Sc in each st across. Ch 1, turn. Rep row 2 for pat st and work even until piece measures 5¾" from beg, end on WS. Ch 1, turn.

Shape Waist

Dec Row (RS): Sc in first 2 sts, [dec 1 st over next 2 sts, sc in next 3 sts] 8 times—34 sts. Work even for 4 rows, end on RS. **Inc Row (WS):** Sc in first 2 sts, [inc 1 st in next st, sc in next 3 sts] 8 times—42 sts. Work even until piece measures 7½" from beg, end on RS. Change to smaller hook, ch 1. Do not turn.

Top Edging

Working from left to right, sc in each st across. Fasten off.

FINISHING

Sew back seam to within ½" of waist shaping.

Right Back Edging

From RS, work 15 sc evenly spaced along right back opening. Ch 1, turn. Work even for 1 more row. Fasten off. Sew 4 bead buttons evenly spaced along left back opening. To close back, push beads between sts of right back edging.

Ruched Accent

Thread needle with A. To accent center front, insert needle, from WS to RS, ½" below top edge. Thread on a bead, then insert needle, from RS to WS through top edging; remove needle. Tie to gather, making a tight knot on WS. Trim off excess yarn.

shrug

With larger hook and B, ch 14. **Row 1:** Dc in 4th ch from hook and in each ch across—11 sts. Ch 3, turn. **Row 2:** Dc in each st across. Ch 3, turn. Rep row 2 for pat st and work even until piece measures 8¼" from beg. Fasten off. Draw in all loose ends. Sew a 2½"-long underarm seam at each end.

Yarn
A Taste of Glitz (25g/190yd) by K1C2, 1 cone #645 Blueberry Swirl (A) and Artic Rays (8yd/7.3m) by Rainbow Gallery, 3 cards #AR14 Bright Blue (B).

Crochet Hooks
Size B (1) and C (2) or sizes to obtain gauges.

Notions
Tapestry needle.
5 dark blue transparent 6/0 "E" beads.

gauges

8 sc = 1" (using larger hook and A).
7 dc = 1" (using larger hook and B).
FOR PROPER FIT, TAKE THE TIME TO CHECK YOUR GAUGES.

"Fur" Frenzy

Feel the need for speed? This fun, faux-fur car coat is perfect for racing around the big city in a sporty convertible. The fly front coat is constructed in one piece using a vibrantly colored, variegated novelty yarn.

car coat

BODY
Made in one piece. Beg at bottom edge, with MC, ch 47. **Row 1 (WS):** Sc in 2nd ch from hook and in each ch across—46 sts. Ch 1, turn. **Row 2:** Sc in each st across. Ch 1, turn. Rep row 2 for pat st and work even until piece measures 3¾" from beg, end on WS. Ch 1, turn.

RIGHT FRONT
Work across first 14 sts. Ch 1, turn. Work even until piece measures 5½" from beg, end on WS. Fasten off.
Back
From RS, sk next st. Join yarn with a sc in next st, sc across next 15 sts— 16 sts. Work even until back measures same length as right front, end on WS. Fasten off.

LEFT FRONT
From RS, sk next st. Join yarn with a sc in next st, sc across last 13 sts— 14 sts. Ch 1, turn. Work even until piece measures same length as right front, end on WS. Fasten off.

SLEEVES
Sew a 4-st shoulder seam each side. From RS, work 23 sc evenly spaced around armhole edge. Ch 1, turn. Work even for 3 more rows, end on WS. Dec 1 st each side on next row, then every 4th row 3 times more— 15 sts. Work even until sleeve measures 3" from beg, end on WS. Fasten off.

FINISHING
Sew sleeve seams.
Collar
From RS, join yarn with a sc in first st of last row of right front, then sc in each st along right front, back and left front—28 sts. Ch 1, turn. Work even for 3 more rows. Fasten off.

materials

Yarn
Dazzle (1oz/116yd) by Prism, 1 hank Cantina.
Crochet Hook
Size C (2) or size to obtain gauge.
Notions
Tapestry needle.

gauge

13 sc and 14 rows = 2".
FOR PROPER FIT, TAKE THE TIME TO CHECK YOUR GAUGE.

Pop Art

Barbie® looks great zipping around town wearing this sparkling yarn combo! The striped hat echoes the bold colorblock motif that adorns the long, v-neck vest. Make the set in single crochet using "Artic Rays" yarn.

vest

BACK

With A, ch 22. **Row 1:** Sc in 2nd ch from hook and in each ch across—21 sts. Ch 1, turn. **Row 2:** Sc in each st across. Ch 1, turn. Rep row 2 for pat st and work even until piece measures 4½" from beg. Fasten off. Turn work.

Armholes

Sk first 2 sts, join A with a sc in next st, work across to within last 2 sts—17 sts. Ch 1, turn. Work even until piece measures 6" from beg. Fasten off.

RIGHT FRONT

With A, ch 11. **Row 1:** Sc in 2nd ch from hook and in each ch across—10 sts. Ch 1, turn. **Row 2:** Sc in each st across. Ch 1, turn. Rep row 2 for pat st and work even for another 8 rows. Join B, ch 1, turn. Work even with B for 10 rows. Join A, ch 1, turn. Work even with A for 10 rows. Join B, ch 1, turn.

Armhole and Front Neck Shaping

Work across first 8 sts. Ch 1, turn. **Next Row:** Work across to within last 2 sts, dec 1 st over last 2 sts (neck edge). Ch 1, turn. **Following Row:** Work even across. Ch 1, turn. Rep these 2 rows twice more—5 sts. Work even until piece measures 6" from beg. Fasten off.

LEFT FRONT

With B, ch 11. **Row 1:** Sc in 2nd ch from hook and in each ch across—10 sts. Ch 1, turn. **Row 2:** Sc in each st across. Ch 1, turn. Rep row 2 for pat st and work even for another 8 rows. Join A, ch 1, turn. Work even with A for 10 rows. Join B, ch 1, turn. Work even with B for 10 rows.

Fasten off. Turn ready for next row.

Armhole and Front Neck Shaping

Sk first 2 sts, join B with a sc in next st, then work across last 7 sts—8 sts. Ch 1, turn. **Next Row:** Dec 1 st over first 2 sts (neck edge), finish row. Ch 1, turn. **Following Row:** Work even across. Ch 1, turn. Rep these 2 rows twice more—5 sts. Work even until piece measures 6" from beg. Fasten off.

FINISHING

Sew shoulder seams. Sew side seams beg just above first color block on each front.

hat

Hat is made from the WS and turned RS out after it is completed. With A, ch 5. Join ch with a sl st forming a ring. **Rnd 1:** Work 6 sc over ch. Mark last st made with the safety pin. You will be working in a spiral marking the last st made with the safety pin to indicate end of rnd. **Rnd 2:** Work 2 sc in each st around—12 sts. **Rnd 3:** * Sc in next st, work 2 sc in next st, rep from * around—18 sts. **Rnd 4:** * Sc in next 2 sts, work 2 sc in next st, rep from * around—24 sts. **Rnd 5:** * Sc in next 3 sts, work 2 sc in next st, rep from * around—30 sts. **Rnds 6-10:** Sc in each st around. After rnd 10 is completed, join B. **Rnds 11-13:** Sc in each st around. After rnd 13 is completed, join rnd with a sl st. Fasten off.

FINISHING

Draw in all loose ends. Turn hat RS out.

materials

Yarn
Artic Rays (8yd/7.3m) by Rainbow Gallery, 7 cards #AR4 Pink (A) and 3 cards #AR7 Silver (B).
Crochet Hook
Size C (2) or size to obtain gauge.
Notions
Tapestry needle. Small safety pin.

note

When changing colors, draw new color through 2 lps on hook to complete sc.

gauge

6 sc = 1".
FOR PROPER FIT, TAKE THE TIME TO CHECK YOUR GAUGE.

Highland Ensemble

This Scottish-inspired ensemble showcases a pocketed shawl and long skirt, both made with alternate rows of single and double crochet. What better way to complete the look than with a matching tam. And you need just one ball of silk and cashmere blend yarn to make all three pieces!

pocket wrap

Wrap is made vertically. Beg at long side edge, ch 91. **Row 1 (WS):** Dc in 4th ch from hook and in each ch across—88 sts. Ch 1, turn. **Row 2 (RS):** Sc in each st across. Ch 3, turn. **Row 3:** Dc in each st across. Ch 1, turn. Rep rows 2 and 3 for pat st. Work even until piece measures 2" from beg, end on WS. Fasten off.
Edging
From RS, join yarn with a sc in side of dc row, work 1 more sc in same dc row. Cont across, working 1 sc in each sc row and 2 sc in each dc row—18 sts. Fasten off. Rep on opposite end.

POCKETS

Make 2. Beg at bottom edge, ch 10. **Row 1:** Sc in 2nd ch from hook and in each ch across—9 sts. Ch 3, turn. **Row 2 (WS):** Dc in each st across. Ch 1, turn. **Row 3 (RS):** Sc in each st across. Ch 3, turn. Rep rows 2 and 3 for pat st. Work even until piece measures 1" from beg, end on WS. Fasten off.

FINISHING

Sew on each pocket, so bottom edge is ½" from bottom edge of wrap and centered side to side.

Fringe

Cut yarn into 3"-lengths. From WS, knot 1 fringe in each sc across each bottom edge. Trim fringe so it measures ¾"-long.

skirt

Skirt is made horizontally in one piece. Beg at bottom edge, ch 44.
Row 1: Sc in 2nd ch from hook and in each ch across—43 sts. Ch 3, turn.
Row 2 (WS): Dc in each st across. Ch 1, turn. **Row 3 (RS):** Sc in each st across. Ch 3, turn. Rep rows 2 and 3 for pat st. Work even until piece measures 4¾" from beg, end on RS. Ch 3, turn.

Shape Waist

Dec Row 1 (WS): Dc in first 3 sts, * dec 1 st over next 2 sts, dc in next 5 sts, rep from * across, end last rep dc in last 3 sts—37 sts. Ch 1, turn.
Dec Row 2: Sc in first 6 sts, * dec 1 st over next 2 sts, sc in next 4 sts, rep from * across, end sc in last st—32 sts. Ch 1, turn. **Dec Row 3:** Sc in first 3 sts, * dec 1 st over next 2 sts, sc in next 4 sts, rep from * across, end last rep, sc in last 3 sts—27 sts. Ch 1, turn. Work even in sc for 3 rows. Fasten off.

FINISHING

Beg 1¾" from bottom edge, sew back seam to within 1¼" of top edge. Sew snap to waist opening.

beret

Ch 3. Join ch with a sl st forming a ring. **Rnd 1:** Work 6 sc over ch. Mark last st made with the safety pin. You will be working in a spiral marking the last st made with the safety pin to indicate end of rnd. **Rnd 2:** Work 2 sc in each st around—12 sts. **Rnd 3:** * Sc in next st, work 2 sc in next st, rep from * around—18 sts. **Rnd 4:** * Sc in next 2 sts, work 2 sc in next st, rep from * around—24 sts. **Rnd 5:** * Sc in next 3 sts, work 2 sc in next st, rep from * around—30 sts. **Rnd 6:** * Sc in next 4 sts, work 2 sc in next st, rep from * around—36 sts. **Rnd 7:** * Sc in next 5 sts, work 2 sc in next st, rep from * around—42 sts. **Rnd 8:** * Sc in next 6 sts, work 2 sc in next st, rep from * around—48 sts. **Rnd 9:** * Sc in next 7 sts, work 2 sc in next st, rep from * around—54 sts. **Rnd 10:** * Sc in next 8 sts, work 2 sc in next st, rep from * around—60 sts. **Rnds 11–13:** Work even around. **Rnd 14:** * Sc in next 4 sts, dec 1 st over next 2 sts, rep from * around—50 sts. **Rnd 15:** * Sc in next 3 sts, dec 1 st over next 2 sts, rep from * around—40 sts. **Rnd 16:** * Sc in next 2 sts, dec 1 st over next 2 sts, rep from * around—30 sts. **Rnd 17:** Work even around. Fasten off.

materials

Yarn
Richesse et Soie
(25g/approx 145yd) by
K1C2, 1 ball #9521 Moss.
Crochet Hook
Size C (2) or size to obtain gauge.
Notions
Tapestry needle.
1 small metal snap.
Small safety pin.

gauge

8 sts and 6 rows = 1"
(in pat st).
FOR PROPER FIT, TAKE THE
TIME TO CHECK YOUR GAUGE.

Springtime Wedding Florals

The perfect gown for the perfect day. This classically styled sleeveless dress has a fitted bodice, v-neck and gently gathered straight skirt. Make the top in single crochet, then add on the skirt which is worked in half double crochet. Complete the look with a sweet garden hat that's trimmed with a circle of dainty crocheted flowers.

wedding gown

FRONT

Beg at bottom edge, ch 21. **Row 1 (WS):** Sc in 2nd ch from hook and in each ch across—20 sts. Ch 1, turn. **Row 2:** Sc in each st across. Ch 1, turn. Rep row 2 for pat st and work even for 1 more row, end on WS.

Shape Sides

Inc 1 st each side on next row, then every other row 6 times more—34 sts. Work even until piece measures 2" from beg, end on WS. Do not ch, turn.

Left Front
Armhole and Neck Shaping

Next Row: Sl st across first 3 sts (armhole edge), ch 1, work across next 12 sts, dec 1 st over next 2 sts (neck edge)—13 sts. Ch 1, turn. **Following Row:** Sc in each st across. Ch 1, turn. Dec 1 st at armhole edge on next row, then every other row once more; AT THE SAME TIME, dec 1 st at neck edge on next row then every other row 6 times more, end on WS—4 sts. Fasten off.

Right Front
Armhole and Neck Shaping

Next Row: From RS, join yarn with a sc in next st, AND AT THE SAME TIME, dec it with next st (neck edge), work across to within last 3 sts (armhole edge)—13 sts. Ch 1, turn. **Following Row:** Sc in each st across. Ch 1, turn. Continue to work same as for left front.

RIGHT BACK

Beg at bottom edge, ch 9. **Row 1 (WS):** Sc in 2nd ch from hook and in each ch across—8 sts. Ch 1, turn. **Row 2:** Sc in each st across. Ch 1, turn. Rep row 2 for pat st and work even for 1 more row, end on WS.

Shape Side

Inc 1 st at beg of next row, then at same edge every other row 6 times more—15 sts. Work even until piece measures 2" from beg, end on WS. Do not ch, turn.

Armhole and Back Neck Shaping

Next Row: Sl st across first 3 sts (armhole edge), ch 1, work across to within last 2 sts, dec 1 st over last 2 sts (neck edge)—11 sts. Ch 1, turn. **Following Row:** Sc in each st across. Ch 1, turn. Dec 1 st at armhole edge once, AT THE SAME TIME, dec 1 st at neck edge on next row then every other row 5 times more—4 sts. Work even until armhole measures same as for front. Fasten off.

materials

WEDDING GOWN
Yarn
Traditions Size 10 Crochet Cotton (400yd/365m) by DMC, 1 ball #B5200 White.
Crochet Hook
Size 4 steel crochet hook or size to obtain gauge.
Notions
Tapestry needle.
Sewing needle.
Beading needle.
White sewing thread.
Beading thread.
3 small metal snaps.
11"-length of ⅛"-wide white satin ribbon.
Mill Hill Seed Beads (4.54g), 1 package #00161 Crystal.
2 bunches (1 dozen per bunch) ¼" white ribbon roses.
White tulle: 7" x 28" (train), 8"-diameter circle (veil) and 1" x 20" strip (bouquet).
1 package Lily Pearl Flower Spray by Wilton Enterprises.
Green floral tape.

note

Top of gown is made first, then side seams are sewn together. The skirt is added on to bottom edge of top and worked in one piece.

gauge

20 sc and 22 rows = 1".
FOR PROPER FIT, TAKE THE TIME TO CHECK YOUR GAUGE.

Springtime Wedding Florals

Embellish the neck, back and frothy tulle train with dozens of the dainty crocheted flowers. Accent each posy with a tiny seed bead.

LEFT BACK

Work same as for right back to side shaping.

Shape Side

Inc 1 st at end of next row, then at same edge every other row 6 times more—15 sts. Work even until piece measures 2" from beg, end on WS. Do not ch, turn.

Armhole and Back Neck Shaping

Next Row: Dec 1 st over first 2 sts (neck edge), work across to within last 3 sts (armhole edge)—11 sts. Ch 1, turn. **Following Row:** Sc in each st across. Ch 1, turn. Dec same as for right front, reversing shaping.

SKIRT

Sew side seams of front and backs. Beg skirt along 36 bottom lps (8 right back, 20 front and 8 left back). From RS, join yarn with a hdc in first bottom lp of right back, * work 2 hdc in next lp, hdc in next lp, rep from * across, end hdc in last st—53 sts. Ch 2, turn. **Following Row:** Hdc in each st across. Ch 2, turn. Rep this row until skirt measures 6" from beg, end on WS. Fasten off.

flowers

(make 36)

Leaving a long end for sewing, ch 4. Join ch with a sl st forming a ring.

Rnd 1: [Ch 4, sc over ring] 6 times. Join rnd with a sl st. Fasten off leaving a long end for sewing. Thread this end into tapestry needle. Insert needle to WS, then run needle through base of sts. Pull tight to gather in center of flower; fasten off securely.

FINISHING

Sew shoulder seams.

Armhole Edging

From RS, join yarn with a sc in side seam, work 23 more sc evenly spaced around entire armhole. Join rnd with a sl st. Fasten off.

Sew skirt seam to within 1" of waist. Cut a 5½"-length of ribbon. Wrap ribbon around waist, folding ends to WS. Sew ribbons ends securely on WS. Sew on 3 snaps evenly spaced along back opening. For train, use sewing needle and thread to run a gathering thread ¼" from one long edge of 7" x 28" tulle. Pull thread to gather tightly; fasten off securely. Sew gathered edge of train to right back, ½" below waistline.

Springtime Wedding Florals

The pretty pastel bridesmaid dresses are all a version of the bride's breathtaking gown. Here, the crocheted blooms accent the neck and back opening only. Matching satin ribbons adorn the waists.

Sew 1 flower to center front neck. Sew 7 flowers along left neck edge, ending at beg of left back neck shaping. Sew 12 flowers, evenly spaced, along right neck edge, ending at right back waist, then continue line of flowers with 4 more flowers along center of train. Sew 12 remaining flowers evenly spaced along hem of train. Using beading needle and thread, sew 1 bead to center of each flower.

hat

Ch 3. Join ch with a sl st forming a ring. **Rnd 1:** Work 6 sc over ch. Mark last st made with the safety pin. You will be working in a spiral marking the last st made with the safety pin to indicate end of rnd. Work through back lps only unless stated otherwise. **Rnd 2:** Work 2 sc in each st around—12 sts. **Rnd 3:** * Sc in next st, work 2 sc in next st, rep from * around—18 sts. **Rnd 4:** * Sc in next 2 sts, work 2 sc in next st, rep from * around—24 sts. **Rnd 5:** * Sc in next 3 sts, work 2 sc in next st, rep from * around—30 sts. **Rnd 6:** * Sc in next 4 sts, work 2 sc in next st, rep from * around—36 sts. **Rnd 7:** * Sc in next 5 sts, work 2 sc in next st, rep from * around—42 sts. **Rnd 8:** * Sc in next 6 sts, work 2 sc in next st, rep from * around—48 sts. **Rnds 9-14:** Sc in each st around.

Brim

Rnd 15: Working through both lps, * sc in next st, work 2 sc in next st, rep from * around—72 sts. Work now though back lps only. **Rnds 16 and 17:** Sc in each st around. **Rnds 18:** * Sc in next 2 sts, work 2 sc in next st, rep from * around—96 sts. **Rnds 19 and 21:** Sc in each st around. After rnd 21 is completed, join rnd with a sl st in next st. Fasten off.

flowers

(make 10)
Make same as for Wedding Gown.

FINISHING

Sew flowers evenly spaced around hat, as shown. Using beading needle and thread, sew 1 seed bead to center of each flower.
Fold tulle circle in half, then in half again to form a one-quarter circle. At back of hat, sew point of circle to WS at base of crown.

materials

BRIDESMAID GOWNS
Yarn
Traditions Size 10 Crochet
Cotton (400yd/365m) by DMC,
1 ball each #5800 Sky Blue
(A), #5211 Lavender (B) and
#5818 Pink (C).
Crochet Hook
Size 4 steel crochet hook or
size to obtain gauge.
Notions
Tapestry needle.
Sewing needle.
Beading needle.
Lt. blue, lavender and pink
sewing threads.
Beading thread.
9 small metal snaps (3 for
each gown).
18"-length of ⅛"-wide, lt.
blue, lavender and pink satin
ribbons.
Mill Hill Seed Bead Mini-Pack
#01005 which includes:
#02005 Dusty Rose (gown A),
#00168 Sapphire (gown B)
and #02001Pearl (gown C).
1/4" ribbon roses (1 dozen per
bunch), 1 bunch each: yellow,
lt. blue, pink and lavender.
Tulle, 1 (1" x 20") strip each:
blue, lavender and pink.
Green floral tape.

note

Top of gown is made first,
then side seams are sewn
together. The skirt is added
on to bottom edge of top
and worked in one piece.

gauge

20 sc and 22 rows = 1".
FOR PROPER FIT, TAKE THE
TIME TO CHECK YOUR GAUGE.

Springtime Wedding Florals

The lovely garden hats are also just like the bride's, but with flowers that are dotted with contrasting color beads. And don't forget the beautiful bouquets made with lots of tiny faux flowers, tulle and ribbon.

bouquet

Gather all ribbon roses together forming a bouquet. Secure stems together with floral tape. Trim stems so handle measures about 1¼"-long. Using sewing needle and thread, run a gathering thread ¼" from one long edge of 1" x 20" tulle. Pull thread to gather forming a circle. Insert handle of bouquet through circle, then pull tight to gather in; fasten circle securely to base of handle.

For streamers, cut remaining ribbon into 3 equal lengths. Sew one end of each streamer to base of handle so they form a fan. Trim free ends of streamers at an angle.

Cut off stems from 2 pearl sprays ¼" from base of pearl loops so loops remain intact. Sew base of loops to base of handle, so they are opposite streamers, as shown.

bridesmaid gowns

Using A, B or C, make same as for Wedding Gown.

flowers

(make 20)
Make same as for Wedding Gown.

FINISHING
Sew shoulder seams.
Armhole Edging
From RS, join yarn with a sc in side seam, work 23 more sc evenly spaced around entire armhole. Join rnd with a sl st. Fasten off.

Sew skirt seam to within 1" of waist. Cut a 5½"-length of matching ribbon. Wrap ribbon around waist, folding ends to WS. Sew ribbons ends securely on WS. Sew on 3 snaps evenly spaced along back opening. Sew 1 flower to center front neck. Sew 12 more flowers, evenly spaced, along right neck edge, ending at right back waist. Sew 7 remaining flowers along left neck edge, ending at beg of left back neck shaping. Using beading needle and thread, sew 1 bead to center of each flower.

hat

With A, B or C, ch 3. Join ch with a sl st forming a ring. **Rnd 1:** Work 6 sc over ch. Mark last st made with the safety pin. You will be working in a spiral marking the last st made with the safety pin to indicate end of rnd. Work through back lps only unless stated otherwise. **Rnd 2:** Work 2 sc in each st around—12 sts. **Rnd 3:** * Sc in next st, work 2 sc in next st, rep from * around—18 sts. **Rnd 4:** * Sc in next 2 sts, work 2 sc in next st, rep from * around—24 sts. **Rnd 5:** * Sc in next 3 sts, work 2 sc in next st, rep from * around—30 sts. **Rnd 6:** * Sc in next 4 sts, work 2 sc in next st, rep from * around—36 sts. **Rnd 7:** * Sc in next 5 sts, work 2 sc in next st, rep from * around—42 sts. **Rnd 8:** * Sc in next 6 sts, work 2 sc in next st, rep from * around—48 sts. **Rnds 9-14:** Sc in each st around.

Brim
Rnd 15: Working through both lps, * sc in next st, work 2 sc in next st, rep from * around—72 sts. Work now though back lps only. **Rnds 16 and 17:** Sc in each st around. **Rnds 18:** * Sc in next 2 sts, work 2 sc in next st, rep from * around—96 sts.
Rnds 19 and 21: Sc in each st around. After rnd 21 is completed, join rnd with a sl st in next st. Fasten off.

flowers

(make 10)
Make same as for Wedding Gown.

FINISHING
Sew flowers evenly spaced around hat, as shown. Using beading needle and thread, sew 1 seed bead to center of each flower.

bouquet

Using all 4 colors, form a mixed bouquet of 16 ribbon roses. Secure stems together with floral tape. Trim stems so handle measures about 1¼"-long. Using sewing needle and thread, run a gathering thread ¼" from one long edge of 1" x 20" tulle. Pull thread to gather forming a circle. Insert handle of bouquet through circle, then pull tight to gather in; fasten circle securely to base of handle.

For streamers, cut remaining ribbon into 3 equal lengths. Gather ends together and sew to base of handle. Cut free ends at an angle, cutting 2 streamers ½" shorter.

Rich Raspberry Ripple Afghan

After a long, hard day at work, nothing's more pleasurable than snuggling on the sofa with a favorite afghan and a good book. Inspired by the "traditional" ripple-stitch afghan, this mini version uses the same increasing and decreasing technique to create the pattern. Four shades of the same color add dynamic interest.

afghan

With 1 ply of A, ch 87. **Row 1:** Sc in 2nd ch from hook and in next 3 ch, * work 3 sc in next ch, sc in next 4 ch, sk next 2 ch, sc in next 4 ch, rep from * across, end work 3 sc in next ch, sc in last 4 ch. Ch 1, turn. Work now through back lps only unless stated otherwise.

Row 2: Sk first sc, * sc in next 4 sts, work 3 sc in next st, sc in next 4 sts, sk next 2 sts, rep from * across to within last 5 sts, end sc in next 3 sts, sk next st, sc through both lps of last st. Join B, ch 1, turn. Rep row 2 for pat st and AT THE SAME TIME, work in the following Stripe Pattern: 2 rows B, 2 rows C, 2 rows D and 2 rows A. Work even until piece measures 10" from beg. Fasten off.

FINISHING
Draw in all loose ends. Using a damp pressing cloth, steam-press lightly to finished measurements.

materials

Yarn
Paternayan 3 Ply Persian Wool (approx 8yd) by JCA, 3 skeins #901 Dk. Pink (A) and 2 skeins each #903 Med. Pink (B), #905 Lt. Pink (C) and #907 Pale Pink (D).
Crochet Hook
Size C (2) or size to obtain gauge.
Notions
Tapestry needle.

size

7¾" x 10".

notes

1. Use 1 ply of yarn throughout.
2. When changing colors, draw new color through 2 lps on hook to complete sc.

gauge

8 sc and 6 rows =1" (in pat st using 1 ply of yarn).
TAKE THE TIME TO CHECK YOUR GAUGE.

Dutch Treat

Traditional granny squares crocheted in traditional delft colors make this afghan and pillow set an heirloom-quality treasure. Although the large and small squares look intricate, they are surprisingly easy to make using a fine wool yarn.

afghan

Make 24 small squares and 6 large squares.

SMALL SQUARE

With A, ch 6. Join ch with a sl st forming a ring. **Rnd 1 (RS):** Ch 3 (always counts as 1 dc), work 2 dc over ring, ch 2, * work 3 dc over ring, ch 2, rep from * 3 times. Join rnd with a sl st in 3rd ch of ch-3. Fasten off. From RS, join B with a sl st in any ch-2 sp. **Rnd 2:** Ch 3, work 2 dc in same ch-2 sp, ch 1, * work (3 dc, ch 2, 3 dc) in next ch-2 sp, ch 1, rep from * 3 times, end with 3 dc in beg ch-2 sp, ch 2. Join rnd with a sl st in 3rd ch of ch-3. Fasten off. From RS, join MC with a sl st in any ch-2 sp. **Rnd 3:** Ch 3, work 2 dc in same ch-2 sp, ch 1, * work 3 dc in next ch-1 sp, ch 1, work (3 dc, ch 2, 3 dc) in next ch-2 sp, ch 1, rep from * 3 times, end with 3 dc in next ch-1 sp, ch 1, 3 dc in beg ch-2 sp, ch 2. Join rnd with a sl st in 3rd ch of ch-3. Fasten off leaving a 10"-long tail for sewing.

LARGE SQUARE

With B, ch 6. Join ch with a sl st forming a ring. **Rnd 1 (RS):** Ch 3 (always counts as 1 dc), work 2 dc over ring, ch 2, * work 3 dc over ring, ch 2, rep from * 3 times. Join rnd with a sl st in 3rd ch of ch-3. Fasten off. From RS, join A with a sl st in any ch-2 sp. **Rnd 2:** Ch 3, work 2 dc in same ch-2 sp, ch 1, * work (3 dc, ch 2, 3 dc) in next ch-2 sp, ch 1, rep from * 3 times, end with 3 dc in beg ch-2 sp, ch 2. Join rnd with a sl st in 3rd ch of ch-3. Fasten off. From RS, join MC with a sl st in any ch-2 sp. **Rnd 3:** Ch 3, work 2 dc in same ch-2 sp, ch 1, * work 3 dc in next ch-1 sp, ch 1, work (3 dc, ch 2, 3 dc) in next ch-2 sp, ch 1, rep from * 3 times, end with 3 dc in next ch-1 sp, ch 1, 3 dc in beg ch-2 sp, ch 2. Join rnd with a sl st in 3rd ch of ch-3. Fasten off. From RS, join B with a sl st in any ch-2 sp. **Rnd 4:** Ch 3, work 2 dc in same ch-2 sp, ch 1, * [work 3 dc in next ch-1 sp, ch 1] twice, work (3 dc, ch 2, 3 dc) in next ch-2 sp, ch 1, rep from * 3 times, end with [work 3 dc in next ch-1 sp, ch 1] twice, 3 dc in beg ch-2 sp, ch 2. Join rnd with a sl st in 3rd ch of ch-3. Fasten off. From RS, join A with a sl st in any ch-2 sp. **Rnd 5:** Ch 3, work 2 dc in same ch-2 sp, ch 1, * [work 3 dc in next ch-1 sp, ch 1] 3 times, work (3 dc, ch 2, 3 dc) in

materials

Yarn
Broder Medicis Tapestry Wool (27.3yd/25m) by DMC, 5 skeins Ecru (MC) and 2 skeins each #8899 Dk. Delft (A) and #8720 Bright Royal Blue (B).

Crochet Hook
Steel crochet hook size 8 or size to obtain gauge.

Notions
Tapestry needle. Small amount of polyester fiberfill.

sizes

Afghan
6" x 8".
Pillow
2" x 2".

gauge

Small square measures 1" x 1" and large square measures 2" x 2". TAKE THE TIME TO CHECK YOUR GAUGE.

Dutch Treat

Make the afghan shown here, or make one large enough to fit any Barbie® doll-size bed by simply making and adding more squares.

next ch-2 sp, ch 1, rep from * 3 times, end with [work 3 dc in next ch-1 sp, ch 1] 3 times, 3 dc in beg ch-2 sp, ch 2. Join rnd with a sl st in 3rd ch of ch-3. Fasten off. From RS, join MC with a sl st in any ch-2 sp.
Rnd 6: Ch 3, work 2 dc in same ch-2 sp, ch 1, * [work 3 dc in next ch-1 sp, ch 1] 4 times, work (3 dc, ch 2, 3 dc) in next ch-2 sp, ch 1, rep from * 3 times, end with [work 3 dc in next ch-1 sp, ch 1] 4 times, 3 dc in beg ch-2 sp, ch 2. Join rnd with a sl st in 3rd ch of ch-3. Fasten off leaving a 10"-long tail for sewing.

FINISHING
Working in groups of 4, sew small squares together forming 6 large squares. Sew squares together to form rows, then sew rows together to form afghan.
Edging
From RS, join MC with a sl st in any ch-2 sp, ch 1, work 2 sc in same ch-2 sp. Sc in each st and ch around, working 3 sc in each ch-2 sp, end with sc in beg ch-2 sp. Join rnd with a sl st in ch-1. Fasten off.

pillow

Make 8 small squares.

FINISHING
Sew 2 groups of 4 squares together to form front and back of pillow.
Edging
Work same as for afghan on both front and back of pillow. With WS facing, whipstitch front and back together leaving last 1" unworked. Stuff pillow with fiberfill; whipstitch opening closed.

Posh Pinwheel Rug

This darling rug is worked from the center out using three pastel shades of baby-weight yarn. Adding fringe around the edge gives it a fun retro look, making it a stylish home accent—perfect for the Barbie® Dream House.

rug

With A, ch 4. Join ch with a sl st forming a ring.

Rnd 1: Work 8 sc over ch. Mark last st made with the safety pin. You will be working in a spiral marking the last st made with the safety pin to indicate end of rnd.

Rnd 2: * With A, sc in next st, with B, sc in same st rep from * around—16 sts. Work now through back lps only.

Rnd 3: * With C, sc in next st, with B, work 2 sc in next st, rep from * around—24 sts.

Rnd 4: * With C, sc in next st, with B, sc in next st, work 2 sc in next st, rep from * around—32 sts.

Rnd 5: * With C, sc in next st, with B, sc in next 2 sts, work 2 sc in next st, rep from * around—40 sts.

Rnd 6: * With C, sc in next st, with B, sc in next 3 sts, work 2 sc in next st, rep from * around—48 sts.

Rnd 7: * With C, sc in next st, with B, sc in next 4 sts, work 2 sc in next st, rep from * around—56 sts.

Rnd 8: * With C, sc in next st, with B, sc in next 5 sts, work 2 sc in next st, rep from * around—64 sts.

Rnd 9: * With C, sc in next st, with B, sc in next 6 sts, work 2 sc in next st, rep from * around—72 sts.

Rnd 10: * With C, sc in next st, with B, sc in next 7 sts, work 2 sc in next st, rep from * around—80 sts.

Rnd 11: * With C, sc in next st, with B, sc in next 8 sts, work 2 sc in next st, rep from * around—88 sts.

Rnd 12: * With C, work 2 sc in next st, with B, sc in next 9 sts, rep from * around—96 sts.

Rnd 13: * With C, sc in next 2 sts, work 2 sc in next st, with B, sc in next 8 sts, rep from * around—104 sts.

Rnd 14: * With C, sc in next 4 sts, work 2 sc in next st, with B, sc in next 7 sts, rep from * around—112 sts.

Rnd 15: * With C, sc in next 6 sts, work 2 sc in next st, with B, sc in next 6 sts, rep from * around—120 sts.

Rnd 16: * With C, sc in next 8 sts, work 2 sc in next st, with B, sc in next 5 sts, rep from * around—128 sts.

Rnd 17: * With C, sc in next 10 sts, work 2 sc in next st, with B, sc in next 4 sts, rep from * around—136 sts.

Rnd 18: * With C, sc in next 12 sts, work 2 sc in next st, with B, sc in next 3 sts, rep from * around—144 sts.

Rnd 19: * With C, sc in next 14 sts, work 2 sc in next st, with B, sc in next 2 sts, rep from * around—152 sts.

Rnd 20: * With C, sc in next 16 sts, work 2 sc in next st, with B, sc in next st, rep from * around—160 sts.

Rnd 21: * With C, sc in next 18 sts, work 2 sc in next st, rep from * around—168 sts. Join rnd with a sl st in next st. Fasten off. Join A with a sl st in any st.

Rnd 22: Working through both lps, sc in each st around. Join rnd with a sl st. Fasten off.

FINISHING
Lightly steam-press rug from WS.
Fringe
Cut yarn into 3"-lengths. From WS, knot 1 fringe in each sc around entire outer edge. Trim fringe so it measures ¾"-long.

materials

Yarn
Jamie Baby (1.75oz/50g) by Lion Brand, 1 skein each #257 Pastel Yellow (A), #201 Pink (B) and #206 Pastel Blue (C).
Crochet Hook
Size C (2) or size to obtain gauge.
Notions
Tapestry needle.
Small safety pin.

notes

1. When changing color, draw new color through 2 lps on hook to complete sc.
2. Work sts over color that's being carried across WS of work to prevent loose strands. Make sure to maintain gauge.

size

Approx 7"-diameter (not including fringe).

gauge

8 sc and 6 rows =1".
TAKE THE TIME TO CHECK YOUR GAUGE.

Sweet Hearts

Bright pastel heart pillows trimmed with white ruffle lace stitch make charming country-chic accents perfect for any Barbie® couch, chair or bed. Make 'em in single crochet using lusturous pearl cotton.

pillow

BACK

With MC, ch 2. **Row 1:** Work 3 sc in 2nd ch from hook. Ch 1, turn. **Row 2:** Sc in each st across. Ch 1, turn. Rep row 2 for pat st and inc 1 st each side every row 7 times—17 sts. Ch 1, turn. Work even for 1 row. Inc 1 st each side on next row, then every other row once more—21 sts. Work even for 2 rows.

Shape Top

Right Half: Work across first 10 sts. Ch 1, turn. Dec 1 st each side every row 3 times—4 sts. Fasten off.

Left Half: Sk center st, join MC with a sc in next st, then work across last 9 sts. Ch 1, turn. Cont to work same as for right half.

FRONT

Make same as for back.

FINISHING

Edging

Place back and front together, edges even. Working through both thicknesses, join CC with a sc in center bottom point. Making sure work lies flat, sc evenly around entire edge, leaving last 1" unworked. Stuff pillow lightly with fiberfill, then cont to sc opening closed, working 2 more sc in center bottom point. Join rnd with a sl st. Do not turn. **Lace Rnd:** Ch 1, * work (2 dc, ch 3, 2 dc) in next st, sk next st, sc in next st, sk next st, rep from * around. Fasten off.

materials

Yarn
Pearl Cotton #5 (25m/27.3yd) by DMC, 1 skein each #604 Lt. Cranberry (MC), #340 Med. Blue Violet (MC) and Blanc (CC).

Crochet Hook
Size B (1) or size to obtain gauge.

Notions
Tapestry needle. Small amount of polyester fiberfill.

size

Approx 3" x 3" (including edging).

gauge

10 sc and 10 rows = 1". TAKE THE TIME TO CHECK YOUR GAUGE.

Fun in the Sun Beachwear

Barbie® makes a big fashion splash wearing a striking striped bikini. Make it in single crochet adding embroidered backstitch stripes after it is completed. Ken® sports trendy colorblock baggies, ideal for walks along the beach or a day of browsing in the marketplace. Worked in single crochet using bright shades of pearl cotton.

striped bikini

Cups

(make 2)

With A, ch 12. **Row 1 (WS):** Sc in 2nd ch from hook and in each ch across—11 sts. Ch 1, turn. **Row 2:** Sc in each st across. Ch 1, turn. Rep row 2 for pat st. Dec 1 st each side on next row, then every other row 3 times more, end on WS—3 sts. **Next Row:** Draw up a lp in next 3 sts, yo and draw through all lps on hook—1 st. Ch 1, turn. **Last Row:** Sc in st. Fasten off.

FINISHING

Assemble top making ties as you go along.

Left Side

With A, ch 35 (left back tie). From RS, work 9 sc evenly spaced along side edge of one cup, ch 29 (left neck tie). Working through bottom lps of ch, sc in 2nd lp from hook and in each of next 27 lps. Work 9 sc evenly spaced along opposite side edge of cup.

Right Side

From RS, work 9 sc evenly spaced along side edge of other cup, ch 29 (right neck tie). Working through bottom lps of ch, sc in 2nd lp from hook and in each of next 27 lps. Work 9 sc evenly spaced along opposite side edge of cup. Ch 36 (right back tie). Working through bottom lps of ch, sc in 2nd lp from hook and in each of next 34 lps.

Bottom Edge

Work 8 sc evenly spaced across bottom edge of each cup. Working through bottom lps of left back tie, sc in 35 lps. Fasten off. Draw in all loose ends.

Embroidered Stripes

On each cup, beg stripes 2 rows from bottom edge. With B, embroider backstiches, working each st around post of a sc st. Rep stripe every 2 rows, as shown.

bottom

Made in one piece. Beg at top back edge, with B, ch 14. **Row 1 (RS):** Sc in 2nd ch from hook and in each ch across—13 sts. Ch 1, turn. **Rows 2-4:** Sc in each st across. Ch 1, turn. **Row 5:** Dec 1 st each side—11 sts. Ch 1, turn. **Rows 6 and 7:** Rep row 2. Ch 1, turn. **Row 8:** Dec 1 st each side—9 sts. Ch 1, turn. **Row 9:** Rep row 2. Ch 1, turn. **Row 10:** Dec 1 st each side—7 sts. Ch 1, turn. **Rows 11-21:** Rep row 2. Ch 1, turn. **Row 22:** Inc 1 st each side—9 sts. Ch 1, turn. **Row 23:** Rep row 2. Ch 1, turn. **Row 24:** Inc 1 st each side—11 sts. Ch 1, turn. **Rows 25 and 26:** Rep row 2. Ch 1, turn. **Row 27:** Inc 1 st each side—13 sts. Ch 1, turn. **Rows 28-30:** Rep row 2. After row 30 has been completed, fasten off.

materials

BIKINI

Yarn

Pearl Cotton #5 (25m/27.3yd) by DMC, 1 skein each #741 Med. Tangerine (A) and #208 Very Dk. Lavender (B).

Crochet Hook

Size B (1) or size to obtain gauge.

Notions

Tapestry needle.

COLOR BLOCK BAGGIES

Yarn

Pearl Cotton #5 (25m/27.3yd) by DMC, 2 skeins each #312 Very Dark Baby Blue (A) and #307 Lemon (B).

Crochet Hook

Size B (1) or size to obtain gauge.

Notions

Tapestry needle.

gauge

10 sc and 10 rows = 1".
FOR PROPER FIT, TAKE THE TIME TO CHECK YOUR GAUGE.

Fun in the Sun Beachwear

Everyone into the pool—and that includes you too, Ken®! These vibrant orange tropical trunks are worked in single crochet and are accented with white racing stripes up the sides and around the bottom edges. An eyelet row, crocheted along the top edge, accommodates the drawstring tie.
A basic solid red bikini is a Barbie® summer wardrobe must-have. Make it in single crochet adding on ties as you add the edgings.

FINISHING
Leg Edging
From RS with B, sc evenly along each side edge making sure work lies flat. Fasten off.
Assemble bottom making waist ties as you go. With B, ch 25. Working through bottom lps of beg ch, work 14 sc along top back edge. Work 14 sc along top front edge, ch 26. **Next Row:** Sc in 2nd ch from hook and in each ch and sc across—78 sts. Fasten off. Draw in all loose ends.

Embroidered Stripes
Beg stripes 2 rows from top front edge. With A, embroider backstiches, working each st around post of a sc st. Rep stripe every 2 rows, as shown.

color block baggies

LEFT SIDE
With A, ch 40. **Row 1 (WS):** Sc in 2nd ch from hook and in each ch across—39 sts. Ch 1, turn. **Row 2:** Sc in each st across. Ch 1, turn. Rep row 2 until piece measures 1¼" from beg, end on WS. Do not ch, turn.

Shape Crotch
Next Row: Sl st across first 3 sts, ch 1, work across to within last 3 st—33 sts. Change to B, ch 1, turn.
Following Row: Work even across. Ch 1, turn. **Next Row:** Dec 1 st each side—31 sts. Ch 1, turn. Work even until piece measures 2¼" from beg, end on WS. Change to A, ch 1, turn.

Waistband
Next Row: Work even across. Ch 1, turn. **Eyelet Row:** Sc in first 2 sts, ch 2, sk next 2 sts, * sc in next st, ch 2, sk next 2 sts, rep from * across, end sc in last 3 sts. Ch 1, turn. **Following Row:** Sc in each sc and work 2 sc over each ch-2 sp. Fasten off.

RIGHT SIDE
Work same as for left side, reversing colors, to eyelet row. **Eyelet Row:** Sc in first 3 sts, ch 2, sk next 2 sts, * sc in next st, ch 2, sk next 2 sts, rep from * across, end sc in last 2 sts. Ch 1, turn. **Following Row:** Sc in each sc and work 2 sc over each ch-2 sp. Fasten off.

FINISHING
Sew front and back seams aligning color blocks. Sew leg seams.
Left Drawstring
With B, ch 46 tightly. Fasten off. Sew one end to inside back seam. Weave drawstring through left side eyelets.
Right Drawstring
Work same as for left using A. Weave drawstring through right side eyelets.

tropical trunks

LEFT SIDE

Beg at bottom edge, with CC, ch 38.
Row 1 (WS): Sc in 2nd ch from hook and in each ch across—37 sc. Ch 1, turn. **Rows 2 and 3:** Sc in each st across. Ch 1, turn. After row 3, join MC, then ch 1 and turn.

Color Pattern

Row 1 (RS): With MC, sc across first 17 sts, join CC, sc across next 3 sts, with MC, sc across last 17 sts. Ch 1, turn. **Row 2:** With MC, sc across first 17 sts, with CC, sc across next 3 sts, with MC, sc across last 17 sts. Ch 1, turn. Rep row 2 for color pat and work even until piece measures ⅞" from beg, end on WS. Do not ch, turn.

Shape Crotch

Next Row: Sl st across first 3 sts, ch 1, keeping to color pat, work across to within last 3 sts—31 sts. Ch 1, turn. **Following Row:** Work even across. Ch 1, turn. **Next Row:** Dec 1 st each side—29 sts. Ch 1, turn. Work even until piece measures 2" from beg, end on WS. Change to CC, ch 1, turn.

Waistband

Next Row: Work even across. Ch 1, turn. **Eyelet Row:** Sc in first 2 sts, ch 2, sk next 2 sts, * sc in next 2 sts, ch 2, sk next 2 sts, rep from * across, end sc in last st. Ch 1, turn.
Following Row: Sc in each sc and work 2 sc over each ch-2 sp. Fasten off.

materials

TROPICAL TRUNKS
Yarn
Pearl Cotton #5 (25m/27.3yd) by DMC, 2 skeins #608 Bright Orange (MC) and 1 skein Blanc (CC).
Crochet Hook
Size B (1) or size to obtain gauge.
Notions
Tapestry needle.

RED BIKINI
Yarn
Pearl Cotton #5 (25m/27.3yd) by DMC, 2 skeins #498 Dk. Red.
Crochet Hook
Size B (1) or size to obtain gauge.
Notions
Tapestry needle.

notes

TROPICAL TRUNKS

1. When changing colors, draw new color through 2 lps on hook to complete sc.
2. Carry color not in use loosely across WS of work.

gauge

10 sc and 10 rows = 1".
FOR PROPER FIT, TAKE THE TIME TO CHECK YOUR GAUGE.

Fun in the Sun Beachwear

The basic bikini is so quick and easy to make, you'll want to make one in each of this summer's hottest colors!

RIGHT SIDE

Work same as for left side, to eyelet row. **Eyelet Row:** Sc in first st, ch 2, sk next 2 sts, * sc in next 2 sts, ch 2, sk next 2 sts, rep from * across, end sc in last 2 sts. Ch 1, turn. **Following Row:** Sc in each sc and work 2 sc over each ch-2 sp. Fasten off.

FINISHING

Sew front and back seams. Sew leg seams.

Drawstring

With CC, tightly crochet a 9¼"-long ch. Fasten off. Beg and ending at center front, weave drawstring through ch-2 sps around waist.

red bikini

Cups
(make 2)

Ch 12. **Row 1 (WS):** Sc in 2nd ch from hook and in each ch across—11 sts. Ch 1, turn. **Row 2:** Sc in each st across. Ch 1, turn. Rep row 2 for pat st. Dec 1 st each side on next row, then every other row 3 times more, end on WS—3 sts. **Next Row:** Draw up a lp in next 3 sts, yo and draw through all lps on hook—1 st. Ch 1, turn. **Last Row:** Sc in st. Fasten off.

FINISHING

Assemble top making ties as you go along.

Left Side

Ch 35 (left back tie). From RS, work 9 sc evenly spaced along side edge of one cup, ch 29 (left neck tie). Working through bottom lps of ch, sc in 2nd lp from hook and in each of next 27 lps. Work 9 sc evenly spaced along opposite side edge of cup.

Right Side

From RS, work 9 sc evenly spaced along side edge of other cup, ch 29 (right neck tie). Working through bottom lps of ch, sc in 2nd lp from hook and in each of next 27 lps. Work 9 sc evenly spaced along opposite side edge of cup. Ch 36 (right back tie). Working through bottom lps of ch, sc in 2nd lp from hook and in each of next 34 lps.

Bottom Edge

Work 8 sc evenly spaced across bottom edge of each cup. Working through bottom lps of left back tie, sc in 35 lps. Fasten off. Draw in all loose ends.

bottom

Made in one piece. Beg at top back edge, ch 14. **Row 1 (RS):** Sc in 2nd ch from hook and in each ch across—13 sts. Ch 1, turn. **Rows 2–4:** Sc in each st across. Ch 1, turn. **Row 5:** Dec 1 st each side—11 sts. Ch 1, turn. **Rows 6 and 7:** Rep row 2. Ch 1, turn. **Row 8:** Dec 1 st each side—9 sts. Ch 1, turn. **Row 9:** Rep row 2. Ch 1, turn. **Row 10:** Dec 1 st each side—7 sts. Ch 1, turn. **Rows 11–21:** Rep row 2. Ch 1, turn. **Row 22:** Inc 1 st each side—9 sts. Ch 1, turn. **Row 23:** Rep row 2. Ch 1, turn. **Row 24:** Inc 1 st each side—11 sts. Ch 1, turn. **Rows 25 and 26:** Rep row 2. Ch 1, turn. **Row 27:** Inc 1 st each side—13 sts. Ch 1, turn. **Rows 28–30:** Rep row 2. After row 30 has been completed, fasten off.

FINISHING
Leg Edging
From RS, sc evenly along each side edge making sure work lies flat. Fasten off.

Assemble bottom making waist ties as you go. Ch 25. Working through bottom lps of beg ch, work 14 sc along top back edge. Work 14 sc along top front edge, ch 26. **Next Row:** Sc in 2nd ch from hook and in each ch and sc across—78 sts. Fasten off. Draw in all loose ends.

Too Cool Tankini

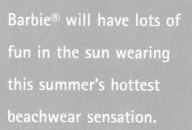

Barbie® will have lots of fun in the sun wearing this summer's hottest beachwear sensation. Perfect for sunbathing by the pool, the set includes a basic black bottom paired with a bright lime green top.

tankini

FRONT

With A, ch 23. **Row 1 (WS):** Sc in 2nd ch from hook and in each ch across—22 sts. Ch 1, turn. **Row 2:** Sc in each st across. Ch 1, turn. Rep row 2 for pat st and AT THE SAME TIME, inc 1 st each side on next row, then every other row 4 times more—32 sts. **Next Row (WS):** Work even across. Fasten off. Turn work.

Bodice

Next Row (RS): Sk first 6 sts, join A with a sc in next st, work across to within last 6 sts—20 sts. Ch 1, turn. **Following Row:** Work even across. Ch 1, turn. Dec 1 st each side on next row, then every other row twice more—14 sts. Ch 1, turn. **Last Row:** Work even across. Fasten off.

LEFT BACK

With A, ch 9. **Row 1 (WS):** Sc in 2nd ch from hook and in each ch across—8 sts. Ch 1, turn. **Row 2:** Sc in each st across. Ch 1, turn. Rep row 2 for pat st and AT THE SAME TIME, inc 1 st at beg of next row, then at same edge every other row 4 times more—13 sts. **Last Row (WS):** Work even across. Fasten off.

RIGHT BACK

Work same as for left back, reversing shaping.

FINISHING

Sew side seams.
Edging and Straps
From RS, join B with a sc in side edge of first row of left back. Making sure that work lies flat, sc evenly along edge to last row of left front. Ch 18 for first strap; fasten off. With B, ch 18 for second strap, then join yarn with a sc in 2nd st of left front top edge. Sc in each st along top front edge to within last st. Ch 18 for third strap; fasten off. With B, ch 18 for fourth strap, then join yarn with a sc in side edge of last row of right front. Making sure that work lies flat, sc evenly along edge to first row of right back. Fasten off. Sew pairs of straps to top back edges, ½" from back opening. Sew on 2 snaps evenly spaced along back opening.

Embroidered Stripes
Beg first of 3 stripes 2 rows down from top front edge. With B, embroider backstiches, working each st around post of a sc st. Rep stripe every 2 rows, as shown.

bottom

Make 2 pieces. With B, ch 31. **Row 1 (WS):** Sc in 2nd ch from hook and in each ch across—30 sts. Ch 1, turn. **Row 2:** Sc in each st across. Do not ch, turn.
Shape Crotch
Next Row: Sl st across first 2 sts, ch 1, sc across to within last 2 sts—26 sts. Ch 1, turn. **Following Row:** Sc across. Ch 1, turn. **Next Row:** Dec 1 st each side—24 sts. Ch 1, turn. Work even in sc until piece measures 1¼" from beg, end on WS. Ch 1, turn.
Shape Waist
Dec Row: Sc across first 3 sts, * dec 1 st over next 2 sts, sc in next 2 sts, rep from * across, end sc in last st—19 sts. Work even until piece measures 1⅝" from beg. Fasten off.

FINISHING
Sew front seam. Sew back seam to within ¾" of top edge. Sew leg seams. Sew a snap to waist opening.

materials

Yarn
Size 5 Perle Cotton (25m/27.3yd) by DMC, 1 skein each #704 Bright Chartreuse (A) and #310 Black (B).
Crochet Hook
Size B (1) or size to obtain gauge.
Notions
Tapestry needle.
3 small metal snaps.

gauge

10 sc and 10 rows = 1".
FOR PROPER FIT, TAKE THE TIME TO CHECK YOUR GAUGE.

Caribbean Beach Cover Up

This sleek and chic hooded coverup works for every summertime activity from shopping at the straw market, to eating conch fritters, to collecting seashells along the beach. Crochet it in one piece using an easy mesh stitch pattern and hot pink pearl cotton.

Yarn
Pearl Cotton #5 (25m/27.3yd) by DMC, 3 skeins #602 Med. Cranberry.
Crochet Hook
Size B (1) or size to obtain gauge.
Notions
Tapestry needle.

body

Made in one piece. Beg at bottom edge, ch 56. **Row 1 (WS):** Dc in 4th ch from hook, * ch 1, sk next ch, dc in next ch, rep from * across—26 ch-1 sps. Ch 3, turn. **Row 2:** Dc in first dc, * ch 1, dc in next dc, rep from * across. Ch 3, turn. Rep row 2 for pat st and work even until piece measures 3½" from beg, end on WS. Ch 3, turn.

Right Front
Work across in pat st until 6 ch 1-sps have been completed, ch 3, turn. Work even until piece measures 4¾" from beg. Fasten off.

Back
Sk next 2 ch-1 sps, join yarn with a sl st in next dc, ch 3, work in pat st across until 10 ch-1 sps have been completed. Ch 3, turn. Work even until piece measures 4¾" from beg. Fasten off.

Left Front
Sk next 2 ch-1 sps, join yarn with a sl st in next dc, ch 3, work in pat st across until 6 ch 1-sps have been completed. Ch 3, turn. Work even until piece measures 4¾" from beg. Fasten off.

hood

Sew a ½" shoulder seam each side.
Foundation Row: From RS, join yarn with a sc in first dc of right front, work 28 more sc along entire neck edge. Ch 3, turn. **Inc Row:** Dc in first st, ch 1, sk next st, * (dc, ch 1, dc) in next st, ch 1, sk next st, [dc in next st, ch 1, sk next st] twice, rep from * across, end (dc, ch 1, dc) in next st, ch 1, sk next st, dc in last st—19 ch-1 sps. Ch 3, turn. Work even in pat st until hood measures 2½" from beg. Fasten off.

FINISHING
Sew hood seam.
Front Edging
From RS, join yarn with a sc over first dc of row 1 of right front, work 1 more sc over same dc, * work 3 sc over each ch-3 turn and 2 sc over each dc, rep from * along entire front edge to bottom of left front. Turn to bottom edge, work 2 sc over each ch-1 sp across. Join rnd with a sl st in first sc. Fasten off.
Armhole Edging
From RS, join yarn with a sc over first ch-1 sp of underarm, work 1 more sc over same ch-1 sp, work 2 sc over next ch-1 sp, * work 3 sc over each ch-3 turn and 2 sc over each dc, rep from * around. Join rnd with a sl st in first sc. Fasten off. Draw in all loose ends.

gauge

5 dc and 4 rows = 1".
FOR PROPER FIT, TAKE THE TIME TO CHECK YOUR GAUGE.

Be My Valentine

Chocolates and flowers...Barbie® wouldn't expect anything less from Ken® on the most romantic day of the year. Here, a lovely light pink pullover accented with a bold white heart motif and dark pink lace-stitch trim. Make the top in no time in single crochet using a soft wool yarn.

pullover

FRONT

Beg at bottom edge, with A, ch 22.
Foundation Row (RS): Sc in 2nd ch from hook and in each ch across—21 sts. Join MC, ch 1, turn.

Chart

Rows 1–6: Sc in each st across. Ch 1, turn. **Row 7 (WS):** Working in sc, beg heart design. Work even until row 13 is completed, end on WS. Do not ch, turn.

Armholes

Row 14 (RS): Sl st across first 2 sts, ch 1, work across to within last 2 sts—17 sts. Ch 1, turn. Work even until row 21 is completed, end on WS. Ch 1, turn.

Shape Left Neck

Row 22: Work across first 6 sts, ch 1, turn. Dec 1 st at neck edge every row twice—4 sts. Work even until row 26 is completed. Fasten off.

Shape Right Neck

Row 22: Sk 5 center sts, join MC with a sc in next st, finish row—6 sts. Ch 1, turn. Dec 1 st at neck edge every row twice—4 sts. Work even until row 26 is completed. Fasten off.

Bottom Edging

From RS, join A with a sc in first bottom lp of beg ch of foundation row, * ch 3, sk next bottom lp, sc in next bottom lp, rep from * across. Fasten off.

BACK

Work same as for front, omitting charted design, until row 13 is completed, end on WS. Do not ch, turn.

Armholes

Sl st across first 2 sts, ch 1, work across to within last 2 sts—17 sts. Ch 1, turn. Work even for 1 row, end on WS. Ch 1, turn.

Divide for Back Opening

Right Half: Work across first 8 sts. Ch 1, turn. Work even until piece measures same length as front. Fasten off. **Left Half:** From RS, sk center st, join MC with a sc in next st, finish row—8 sts. Cont to work same as for right half.

Bottom Edging

Work same as for front.

SLEEVES

Sew shoulder seams. From RS with MC, work 21 sc evenly spaced along armhole edge. Work even in sc for 1", end on WS. Dec 1 st each side on next row, then every 4th row 3 times more—13 sts. Work even until

sleeve measures 3" from beg, end on WS. Join A, ch 1, turn.

Edging

Row 1: Sc in each st across. Ch 1, turn. **Row 2:** Sc in first st, * ch 3, sk next st, sc in next st, rep from * across. Fasten off.

FINISHING

Lightly steam-press pullover. Sew side and sleeve seams.

Neck Edging

From RS with MC, work 25 sc evenly spaced along entire neck edge. Join A, ch 1, turn. Rep rows 1 and 2 same as for sleeve. Fasten off. Sew snap to top of back neck opening.

materials

Yarn

Paternayan 3 Ply Persian Wool (approx 8yd) by JCA, 3 skeins #945 Lt. Pink (MC) and 1 skein each #904 Dk. Pink (A) and #260 White (B).

Crochet Hook

Size C (2) or size to obtain gauge.

Notions

Tapestry needle.
1 small metal snap.

notes

1. Use 1 ply of yarn throughout.
2. When changing colors, draw new color through 2 lps on hook to complete sc.
3. Carry color not in use loosely across WS of work.
4. When working across more than 5 sts, use a separate strand of MC.

gauge

7 sc and 10 rows = 1" (using 1 ply of yarn).
FOR PROPER FIT, TAKE THE TIME TO CHECK YOUR GAUGE.

Color Key
- Lt. Pink MC
- White B

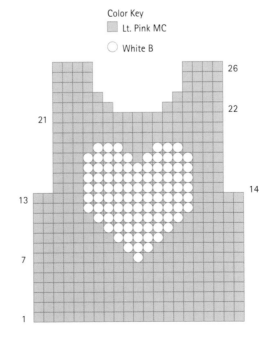

Festive Holiday Dress-Ups

Ho, ho, ho! Join Santa's helpers in spreading Yuletide cheer—it'll be the best Christmas ever. Ken® doll's four-piece traditional Santa suit is detailed down to the coal black buttons and shiny gold belt buckle. Barbie® wears a merry mini dress that fastens closed with little gold bead buttons.

SANTA SUIT
Yarn
Richesse et Soie (25g/approx 145yd) by K1C2, 2 balls #9359 Pimento (MC) and 1 ball #9900 Jet (A), and Artic Rays (8yd/7.3m) by Rainbow Gallery, 2 cards #AR2 White (B).
Crochet Hooks
Size B (1) and C (2) or size to obtain gauge.

Notions
Tapestry needle.
5 (1/8") black Doll Buttons #13056 by JHB International.
1 (3/8") gold Doll Buckle #930 by JHB International.
1 (10mm) white acrylic pompom.
Elastic thread.
Small safety pin.

santa suit

BACK

Beg at bottom edge, with larger hook and MC, ch 25. **Row 1 (WS):** Sc in 2nd ch from hook and in each ch across—24 sts. Ch 1, turn. **Row 2:** Sc in each st across. Ch 1, turn. Rep row 2 for pat st and work even until piece measures 2½" from beg, end on WS. Do not ch, turn.

Armholes

Sl st across first 2 sts, ch 1, work across to within last 2 sts—20 sts. Ch 1, turn. Work even until piece measures 4¼" from beg. Fasten off.

LEFT FRONT

With larger hook and MC, ch 15. **Row 1 (WS):** Sc in 2nd ch from hook and in each ch across—14 sts. Ch 1, turn. **Row 2:** Sc in each st across. Ch 1, turn. Rep row 2 for pat st and work even until piece measures 2½" from beg, end on WS. Do not ch, turn.

Armhole

Sl st across first 2 sts—12 sts. Work even until piece measures 3⅝" from beg, end on WS.

Shape Neck

Work across first 8 sts, ch 1, turn. Dec 1 st at neck edge on next row, then every row twice more—5 sts. Work even until piece measures 4¼" from beg. Fasten off.

note

When changing colors, draw new color through 2 lps on hook to complete sc.

gauge

8 sc and 10 rows = 1" (using larger hook and MC). FOR PROPER FIT, TAKE THE TIME TO CHECK YOUR GAUGE.

Festive Holiday Dress-Ups

Make both outfits in basic single crochet using a bright red cashmere blend yarn. Trim collars and cuffs with snowy white, faux-fur novelty yarn and top the stocking caps with tiny pompoms.

RIGHT FRONT

Work same as for left front until piece measures 2½" from beg, end on WS. Ch 1, turn.

Armhole

Work across to within last 2 sts. Ch 1, turn. Work even until piece measures 3⅝" from beg, end on WS. Do not ch, turn.

Shape Neck

Sl st across first 4 sts, ch 1, finish row—8 sts. Ch 1, turn. Cont to work same as for left front.

SLEEVES

Sew shoulder seams. From RS, with larger hook and MC work 28 sc evenly spaced along armhole edge. Ch 1, turn. Work even in sc until sleeve measures ¾" from beg, end on WS. Dec 1 st each side on next row, then every 4th row 5 times more—16 sts. Work even until sleeve measures 3⅜" from beg, end on WS. Join B, ch 1, turn. Work even for 4 rows. Fasten off.

FINISHING

Sew side and sleeve seams. Turn up cuffs.

Collar

From RS, sk first 2 sts of right front neck shaping. With larger hook, join B with a sc in next st, then work 24 more sc evenly spaced across neck edge to within last 2 sts of left neck shaping—25 sts. Ch 1, turn. Work even in sc for 5 more rows. Fasten off.

On right front, sew 1 black button just below beg of neck shaping, then another ¼" from bottom edge. Sew 3 more buttons evenly spaced between. To close jacket, push buttons between sts.

belt

With smaller hook and A, ch 4. **Row 1:** Sc in 2nd ch from hook and in each ch across—3 sts. Ch 1, turn. **Row 2:** Sc in each st across. Ch 1, turn. Rep row 2 until piece measures 6" from beg. Fasten off.

FINISHING

Draw in all loose ends. Sew buckle to belt.

pants

Make 2 pieces. Beg at bottom edge, with larger hook and MC, ch 25. **Row 1 (WS):** Sc in 2nd ch from hook and in each ch across—24 sts. Ch 1, turn. **Row 2:** Sc in each st across. Ch 1, turn. Rep row 2 for pat st and work even until leg measures 2½" from beg, end on WS.

Shape Leg

Inc 1 st each side on next row, then every 6th row 3 times more—32 sts. Work even until leg measures 5" from beg, end on WS. Do not ch, turn.

Shape Crotch

Sl st across first 2 sts, ch 1, work across to within last 2 sts—28 sts. Ch 1, turn. Work even for 1 row. Dec 1 st each side of next row, then every row once more—24 sts. Ch 1, turn. Work even until leg measures 6¼" from beg, end on WS. Fasten off.

FINISHING

Sew front and back seam. Sew leg seams. Weave elastic thread through last row; fasten off securely.

cap

With larger hook and MC, ch 4. Join ch with a sl st forming a ring. **Rnd 1:** Work 6 sc over ch. Mark last st made with the safety pin. You will be working in a spiral marking the last st made with the safety pin to indicate end of rnd. **Rnds 2 and 3:** Sc in each st around. **Rnd 4:** [Sc in next st, work 2 sc in next st] 3 times—9 sts. **Rnds 5 and 6:** Rep rnd 2. **Rnd 7:** [Sc in next 2 sts, work 2 sc in next st] 3 times—12 sts. **Rnds 8 and 9:** Rep rnd 2. **Rnd 10:** [Sc in next 3 sts, work 2 sc in next st] 3 times—15 sts. **Rnds 11 and 12:** Rep rnd 2. **Rnd 13:** [Sc in next 4 sts, work 2 sc in next st] 3 times—18 sts. **Rnds 14 and 15:** Rep rnd 2. **Rnd 16:** [Sc in next 5 sts, work 2 sc in next st] 3 times—21 sts. **Rnds 17 and 18:** Rep rnd 2. **Rnd 19:** [Sc in next 6 sts, work 2 sc in next st] 3 times—24 sts. **Rnds 20 and 21:** Rep rnd 2. **Rnd 22:** [Sc in next 7 sts, work 2 sc in next st] 3 times—27 sts. **Rnds 23 and 24:** Rep rnd 2. **Rnd 25:** [Sc in next 8 sts, work 2 sc in next st] 3 times—30 sts. **Rnds 26 and 27:** Rep rnd 2. **Rnd 28:** [Sc in next 9 sts, work 2 sc in next st] 3 times—33 sts. **Rnds 29-32:** Rep rnd 2. After rnd 32 is completed, join B.
Brim
Rnds 33-36: Rep rnd 2. After rnd 36 is completed, join rnd with a sl st in next st. Fasten off.

FINISHING
Sew pomom to top of cap. Fold up brim. Fold top of cap over and tack in place, as shown.

santa dress

Made in one piece. Beg at bottom edge, with MC, ch 55. **Row 1 (WS):** Sc in 2nd ch from hook and in each ch across—54 sts. Ch 1, turn. **Row 2:** Sc in each st across. Ch 1, turn. Rep row 2 for pat st and work even until piece measures 1¾" from beg, end on WS. Ch 1, turn.

Shape Waist

Dec Row 1: Sc in first 5 sts, [dec 1 st over next 2 sts, sc in next 4 sts] 8 times, end sc in last st—46 sts. Ch 1, turn. **Following Row:** Sc in each st across. Ch 1, turn. **Dec Row 2:** Sc in first 5 sts, [dec 1 st over next 2 sts, sc in next 3 sts] 8 times, end sc in last st—38 sts. Ch 1, turn. **Following Row:** Sc in each st across. Ch 1, turn. **Dec Row 3:** Sc in first 4 sts, [dec 1 st over next 2 sts, sc in next 2 sts] 8 times, end sc in last 2 sts—30 sts. Ch 1, turn. **Next 3 Rows:** Sc in each st across. Ch 1, turn. **Inc Row 1:** Sc in first 4 sts, [work 2 sc in next st, sc in next 2 sts] 8 times, end sc in last 2 sts—38 sts. Ch 1, turn. **Following Row:** Sc in each st across. Ch 1, turn. **Inc Row 2:** Sc in first 4 sts, [work 2 sc in next st, sc in next 3 sts] 8 times, end sc in last 2 sts—46 sts. Ch 1, turn. **Next 7 Rows:** Sc in each st across. Ch 1, turn.

Right Front

Work across first 12 sts, ch 1, turn. Work even until right front measures 5" from beg, end on WS. Do not ch, turn.

materials

SANTA DRESS AND CAP
Yarn
Richesse et Soie (25g/approx 145yd) by K1C2, 1 ball #9359 Pimento (MC) and Artic Rays (8yd/7.3m) by Rainbow Gallery, 2 cards #AR2 White (CC).
Crochet Hook
Size C (2) or size to obtain gauge.
Notions
Tapestry needle.
6 (4mm) gold pearls.
1 (10mm) white acrylic pompom.
Small safety pin.

note

When changing colors, draw new color through 2 lps on hook to complete sc.

gauge

8 sc and 10 rows = 1" (using MC).
FOR PROPER FIT, TAKE THE TIME TO CHECK YOUR GAUGE.

Festive Holiday Dress-Ups

These wonderful ensembles are sure to be the hit of the season!

Shape Neck

Sl st across first 4 sts, ch 1, work across last 8 sts. Dec 1 st at neck edge on next row, then every row twice more—5 sts. Fasten off.

BACK

From RS, sk next 2 sts. Join MC with a sc in next st, then sc in next 17 sts—18 sts. Ch 1, turn. Work even until back measures same length as right front to shoulders. Fasten off.

Left Front

From RS, sk next 2 sts. Join MC with a sc in next st, then sc in next 11 sts—12 sts. Ch 1, turn. Work even until left front measures 5" from beg, end on WS.

Shape Neck

Work across first 8 sts, ch 1, turn. Dec 1 st at neck edge on next row, then every row twice more—5 sts. Fasten off.

SLEEVES

Sew shoulder seams. From RS, with MC, work 26 sc evenly spaced along armhole edge. Ch 1, turn. Work even in sc until sleeve measures ¾" from beg, end on WS. Dec 1 st each side on next row, then every 4th row 4 times more—16 sts. Work even until sleeve measures 3" from beg, end on WS. Join CC, ch 1, turn. Work even for 4 rows. Fasten off.

FINISHING

Sew sleeve seams. Turn up cuffs.

Collar

From RS, sk first 3 sts of right front neck shaping, join CC with a sc in next st, then work 17 more sc evenly spaced across neck edge to within last 3 sts of left neck shaping—18 sts. Ch 1, turn. Work even in sc for 5

more rows. Fasten off.
On left front, sew 1 gold pearl just below beg of neck shaping, then 5 more spaced ⁵⁄₈" apart. To close dress, push pearls between sts.

cap

With MC, ch 4. Join ch with a sl st forming a ring. **Rnd 1:** Work 6 sc over ch. Mark last st made with the safety pin. You will be working in a spiral marking the last st made with the safety pin to indicate end of rnd. **Rnds 2 and 3:** Sc in each st around. **Rnd 4:** [Sc in next st, work 2 sc in next st] 3 times—9 sts. **Rnds 5 and 6:** Rep rnd 2. **Rnd 7:** [Sc in next 2 sts, work 2 sc in next st] 3 times—12 sts. **Rnds 8 and 9:** Rep rnd 2. **Rnd 10:** [Sc in next 3 sts, work 2 sc in next st] 3 times—15 sts. **Rnds 11 and 12:** Rep rnd 2. **Rnd 13:** [Sc in next 4 sts, work 2 sc in next st] 3 times—18 sts. **Rnds 14 and 15:** Rep rnd 2. **Rnd 16:** [Sc in next 5 sts, work 2 sc in next st] 3 times—21 sts. **Rnds 17 and 18:** Rep rnd 2. **Rnd 19:** [Sc in next 6 sts, work 2 sc in next st] 3 times—24 sts. **Rnds 20 and 21:** Rep rnd 2. **Rnd 22:** [Sc in next 7 sts, work 2 sc in next st] 3 times—27 sts. **Rnds 23 and 24:** Rep rnd 2. **Rnd 25:** [Sc in next 8 sts, work 2 sc in next st] 3 times—30 sts. **Rnds 26 and 27:** Rep rnd 2. **Rnd 28:** [Sc in next 9 sts, work 2 sc in next st] 3 times—33 sts. **Rnds 29-32:** Rep rnd 2. After rnd 32 is completed, join CC.

Brim

Rnds 33–36: Rep rnd 2. After rnd 36 is completed, join rnd with a sl st in next st. Fasten off.

FINISHING
Sew pompom to top of cap. Fold up brim. Fold top of cap over and tack in place, as shown.

Jolly Jack-'O-Lantern

From witches and vampires to ghosts and goblins, Barbie® welcomes little trick-or-treaters at her doorstep. Worked in single-ply wool, her delightful pumpkin pullover is a wonderful holiday crocheted fashion that sports contrasting ribbed hem, cuffs and turtleneck.

pullover

FRONT

Ribbing: Ribbing is made vertically. With smaller hook and CC, ch 6. **Row 1:** Sc in 2nd ch from hook and in each ch across—5 sts. Ch 1, turn. **Row 2:** Working through back lps only, sc in each st across. Ch 1, turn. Rep row 2 for rib pat and work even until piece measures 2¾" from beg. Ch 1, turn to long edge of ribbing.

Foundation Row (WS): Work 23 sc evenly spaced across long edge of ribbing. Change to larger hook. Join MC, ch 1, turn.

Chart

Rows 1–5: Sc in each st across. Ch 1, turn. **Row 6 (WS):** Working in sc, beg face design. Work even until row 13 is completed, end on RS. Do not ch, turn.

Armholes

Row 14 (WS): Sl st across first 2 sts, ch 1, work across to within last 2 sts—19 sts. Ch 1, turn. Work even until row 20 is completed, end on WS. Ch 1, turn.

Shape Left Neck

Row 21 (RS): Work across first 7 sts, ch 1, turn. Dec 1 st at neck edge every row twice—5 sts. Work even until row 26 is completed. Fasten off.

Shape Right Neck

Row 21 (RS): Sk 5 center sts, join MC with a sc in next st, finish row—7 sts. Ch 1, turn. Dec 1 st at neck edge every row twice—5 sts. Work even until row 26 is completed. Fasten off.

BACK

Work same as for front, omitting charted design, until row 13 is completed, end on RS. Do not ch, turn.

Armholes

Sl st across first 2 sts, ch 1, work across to within last 2 sts—19 sts. Ch 1, turn. Work even for 2 rows, end on WS. Ch 1, turn.

Divide for Back Opening

Right Half: Work across first 9 sts. Ch 1, turn. Work even until piece measures same as length as front to shoulders. Fasten off. **Left Half:** From RS, sk center st, join MC with a sc in next st, finish row—9 sts. Cont to work same as for right half.

SLEEVES

Ribbing: With smaller hook and CC, ch 5. **Row 1:** Sc in 2nd ch from hook and in each ch across—4 sts.

Ch 1, turn. **Row 2:** Working through back lps only, sc in each st across. Ch 1, turn. Rep row 2 for rib pat and work even until piece measures 1½" from beg. Ch 1, turn to long edge of ribbing. **Foundation Row (WS):** Work 18 sc evenly spaced across long edge of ribbing. Change to larger hook. Join MC, ch 1, turn. Work even in sc for 1", end on WS. Inc 1 st each side on next row, then every 10th row once more—22 sts. Work even until sleeve measures 3" from beg, end on WS. Fasten off.

FINISHING

Lightly steam-press pieces. Sew shoulder seams. Sew on sleeves. Sew side and sleeve seams.

Turtleneck

Ribbing: With smaller hook and CC, ch 12. **Row 1:** Sc in 2nd ch from hook and in each ch across—11 sts. Ch 1, turn. **Row 2:** Working through back lps only, sc in each st across. Ch 1, turn. Rep row 2 for rib pat and work even until piece measures 4¼" from beg. Fasten off. Sew turtleneck to neck edge. Sew 1 snap to top of back neck opening and 1 snap to turtleneck.

Color Key

■ Orange MC
● Black CC

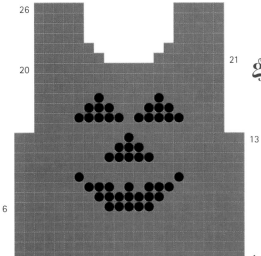

materials

Yarn
Paternayan 3 Ply Persian Wool (approx 8yd) by JCA, 3 skeins #810 Orange (MC) and 2 skeins #220 Black (CC).

Crochet Hooks
Size B (1) and C (2) or size to obtain gauge.

Notions
Tapestry needle.
2 small metal snaps.

notes

1. Use 1 ply of yarn throughout.
2. When changing colors, draw new color through 2 lps on hook to complete sc.
3. Carry color not in use loosely across WS of work.

gauge

7 sc and 10 rows = 1" (using 1 ply of yarn and larger hook). FOR PROPER FIT, TAKE THE TIME TO CHECK YOUR GAUGE.

Wedding Splendor

Something old, something new, something borrowed and something blue... Barbie® makes a stunning bride in a graceful gown resplendent with iridescent pearls.

top

STITCH GLOSSARY

P st = pearl st. Worked on WS rows. Insert hook into st. Slide a pearl all the way up lead yarn to hook. Going under lead yarn, hook lead yarn that's coming out of left side of pearl and draw up a lp. Yo and draw through both lps on hook.

FRONT

Using flexible needle, string 162 pearls onto yarn. Beg at bottom edge, ch 24. **Foundation Row (RS):** Sc in 2nd ch from hook and in each ch across—23 sts. Ch 1, turn.

Pearl Stitch Pattern

Row 1 (WS): Sc in first st, * P st in next st, sc in next st, rep from * across, end P st in last st. Ch 1, turn. **Row 2:** Sc in each st across. Ch 1, turn. **Row 3 (WS):** Sc in first 2 sts, * P st in next st, sc in next st, rep from * across. Ch 1, turn. **Row 4:** Sc in each st across. Ch 1, turn. Rep rows 1-4 for pat st. AT THE SAME TIME, when 5 pat st rows have been completed from beg, end on WS.

Shape Sides

Keeping to pat st, inc 1 st each side on next row, then every 4th row twice more—29 sts. Work even until piece measures 1½" from beg, end on WS. Do not ch, turn.

Armholes

Sl st across first 3 sts, ch 1, work across to within last 3 sts—23 sts. Ch 1, turn. **Following Row:** Work even across. Ch 1, turn. Dec 1 st each side on next row, then every

other row once more, end on WS—19 sts. Ch 1, turn. Work even until piece measures 2½" from beg, end on WS. Ch 1, turn.

Shape Left Neck

Work across first 7 sts, ch 1, turn. Dec 1 st at neck edge on next row, then every row once more—5 sts. Work even for 3 more rows. Fasten off.

Shape Right Neck

From RS, sk 5 center sts, join yarn with a sc in next st, work across last 6 sts—7 sts. Cont to shape neck same as for left side.

RIGHT BACK

Using flexible needle, string 70 pearls onto yarn. Beg at bottom edge, ch 12. **Foundation Row (RS):** Sc in 2nd ch from hook and in each ch across—11 sts. Ch 1, turn. Work in pat st same as for front and work even until 5 pat st rows have been completed from beg, end on WS.

Shape Side

Keeping to pat st, inc 1 st at beg of next row, then at same edge every 4th row twice more—14 sts. Work even until piece measures 1½" from beg, end on WS. Do not ch, turn.

Armhole

Keeping to pat st, sl st across first 3 sts, ch 1, finish row—11 sts. Ch 1, turn. **Following Row:** Work even across. Ch 1, turn. **Next Row:** Dec 1 st at armhole edge once—10 sts. Ch 1, turn. Work even until back measures same length as front. Fasten off.

materials

Yarn
Cebelia Size 10 Crochet Cotton (260m/284yd) by DMC, 1 ball #0002 Ecru.

Crochet Hook
Size B (1) crochet hook or size to obtain gauge.

Notions
Tapestry needle.
Sewing needle.
Flexible Magnetic Needle.
Ecru sewing thread.
4 small metal snaps.
Small safety pin.
528 (3mm) ecru pearls.
Ecru tulle: 11" x 33" rectangle (veil) and 2" x 15" strip (bouquet).
20"-length of ⅛"-wide ecru satin ribbon.
12 miniature polymer clay calla lilies (each flower head approx ⅝"-long) or any similar size clay or silk flowers.
Green floral tape.

note

Pearl st pat is based on alternating rows of pearls forming a diagonal pat. To keep to pat st when working inc and dec, be sure that pearls cont to alternate. For best results, turn to RS after making a couple of pearl sts to make sure that pearls alternate with those of row below.

gauge

9 sts and 10 rows = 1" (in pat st).
FOR PROPER FIT, TAKE THE TIME TO CHECK YOUR GAUGE.

Wedding Splendor

The sleeveless fitted top is encrusted with pearls, while the long, slim skirt is simply dotted with them. The pillbox hat with a floor-length veil offers a stylish twist on tradition. This beautiful ensemble is a forever keepsake to pass on from generation to generation.

LEFT BACK

Work same as for right back to side shaping.

Shape Side

Keeping to pat st, inc 1 st at end of next row, then at same edge every 4th row twice more—14 sts. Work even until piece measures 1½" from beg, end on WS. Ch 1, turn.

Armhole

Work across first 11 sts, ch 1, turn. **Following Row:** Work even across. Ch 1, turn. **Next Row:** Dec 1 st at armhole edge once—10 sts. Ch 1, turn. Work even until back measures same length as front.

FINISHING

Sew shoulder and side seams.

Armhole Edging

From RS, join yarn with a sc in side seam, work 25 more sc evenly spaced around entire armhole. Join rnd with a sl st. Fasten off.

Collar

Using flexible needle, string 23 pearls onto yarn. From RS, join yarn with a sc in first st of left back neck edge, then work 24 more sc evenly spaced to last st of right back neck edge—25 sts. Ch 1, turn. Work pat st rows 1-4 same as for front. Fasten off.

Right Back Edging

From RS, join yarn with a sc in side edge of last row of collar. Making sure that work lies flat, sc evenly along edge to first row of right back. Ch 1, turn. Work even for 1 more row. Fasten off.

Left Back Edging

From RS, join yarn with a sc in side edge of first row of left back. Making sure that work lies flat, sc evenly along edge to last row of collar. Ch 1, turn. Work even for 1 more row. Fasten off. Sew 3 snaps evenly spaced along back opening, so edges overlap ¼".

SKIRT

Made in one piece. Using flexible needle, string 112 pearls onto yarn. Beg at bottom edge, ch 45.

Foundation Row: Sc in 2nd ch from hook and in each ch across—44 sts. Ch 1, turn.

Pearl Stitch Pattern

Row 1 (WS): Sc in first 2 sts, * P st in next st, sc in next 5 sts, rep from * across. Ch 1, turn. **Rows 2, 3 and 4:** Sc in each st across. Ch 1, turn. **Row 5 (WS):** * Sc in next 5 sts, P st in next st, rep from * across, end sc in last 2 sts. Ch 1, turn. **Rows 6, 7 and 8:** Sc in each st across. Ch 1, turn. Rep rows 1-8, 6 times more, then rows 1-5 once more, end on WS.

Shape Waist

Dec Row 1 (RS): Sc in first 2 sts [dec 1 st over next 2 sts, sc in next 4 sts] 7 times—37 sts. Ch 1, turn. **Following Row:** Sc in each st across. Ch 1, turn. **Dec Row 2:** Sc in first 2 sts, [dec 1 st over next 2 sts, sc in next 3 sts] 7 times—30 sts. Ch 1, turn. Work even in sc for 3 more rows. Fasten off.

FINISHING

Sew back seam to within 1" of top edge. Sew 1 snap to waist opening.

pillbox hat

Using flexible needle, string 70 pearls onto yarn. Ch 3. Join ch with a sl st forming a ring. **Rnd 1:** Work 6 sc over ch. Mark last st made with the safety pin. You will be working in a spiral marking the last st made with the safety pin to indicate end of rnd. **Rnd 2:** Work 2 sc in each st around—12 sts. **Rnd 3:** * Sc in next st, work 2 sc in next st, rep from * around—18 sts. **Rnd 4:** * Sc in next 2 sts, work 2 sc in next st, rep from * around—24 sts. **Rnd 5:** * Sc in next 3 sts, work 2 sc in next st, rep from * around—30 sts. **Rnd 6:** * Sc in next 4 sts, work 2 sc in next st, rep from * around—36 sts. Ch 1, turn. Working back and forth in rows, work in pearl pat st same as for front of top until rows 1-4 have been worked twice. Fasten off.

FINISHING
Sew back seam. Using sewing needle and thread, sew a pearl to center top of hat.

veil

Using sewing needle and thread, run a gathering thread $\frac{1}{4}$" from one long edge of 11" x 33" tulle. Pull thread to gather, making sure edge measures $1\frac{1}{2}$"-wide. Fasten off securely. Pin gathered edge to inside of hat, centering veil at back seam. Sew veil in place.

bouquet

Gather flowers stems together, then arrange flower heads, as shown. Tightly wrap stems together with floral tape to secure bouquet. Trim stems, if necessary, so that handle measures about $1\frac{1}{2}$"-long. Curve taped stems to form handle. For streamers, cut a 9"-length of ribbon; trim both ends at an angle. Fold ribbon so that one end is 1" longer than the other. Using sewing needle and thread, tack fold to base of handle. On one side of each streamer, sew 10 pearls evenly spaced. Form remaining ribbon into 3 ($1\frac{1}{2}$"-long) loops. Tack base of loops to base of handle. Run a gathering thread $\frac{1}{4}$" from one long edge of 2" x 15" tulle. Pull thread tight to gather forming a collar; fasten off securely. Fold corners of free ends to center of collar and tack to secure. Sew center of collar to base of handle, so folded ends are at top.

Classic Suit Ensemble

This timeless two-piece suit, with a matching pillbox hat and shoulder bag, embraces the true sophistication and elegance of a bygone era. Every detail is addressed from the gold ball buttons to the woven gold chain strap.

jacket

BACK

With CC, ch 23. **Row 1 (RS):** Sc in 2nd ch from hook and in each ch across—22 sts. Ch 1, turn. **Row 2:** Sc in each st across. Change to MC, ch 1, turn. **Row 3:** Rep row 2. Ch 1, turn. **Pattern St—Row 1:** * Sc in next st, dc in next st, rep from * across. Ch 1, turn. Rep this row until piece measures 1¾" from beg, end on WS. Do not ch, turn.

Armholes

Sl st across first 3 sts, ch 3, work across to within last 3 sts—16 sts. Ch 3, turn. Keeping to pat st as described in Note 3, work even until piece measures 3⅛" from beg. Fasten off.

LEFT FRONT

With CC, ch 15. **Row 1 (RS):** Sc in 2nd ch from hook and in each ch across—14 sts. Ch 1, turn. **Row 2:** Sc in each st across. Change to MC, ch 1, turn. **Row 3 (RS):** With MC, sc across first 12 sts, with CC, sc across last 2 sts. Ch 2, turn. **Row 4:** With CC, hdc in first 2 sts, with MC, [sc in next st, dc in next st] 6 times. Ch 1, turn. **Row 5:** With MC, [sc in next st, dc in next st] 6 times, with CC, hdc in last 2 sts. Ch 2, turn. Rep rows 4 and 5 for pat st and front band and work even until piece measures 1¾" from beg, end on WS. Do not ch, turn.

Armhole

Next Row (RS): Sl st across first 3 sts, ch 3, work across last 11 sts. Keeping to pat st (as described in Note 3) and front band as established, work even until piece measures 1¾" from beg, end on WS.

Shape Neck

Next Row (RS): Work across first 6 sts, ch 1, turn. Fasten off CC. Keeping to pat st, dec 1 st at neck edge on next row, then every row once more—4 sts. Work even until front measures same length as back. Fasten off.

RIGHT FRONT

With CC, ch 15. **Row 1 (RS):** Sc in 2nd ch from hook and in each ch across—14 sts. Ch 1, turn. **Row 2:** Sc in each st across. Ch 1, turn. **Row 3 (RS):** With CC, sc across first 2 sts, join MC, then sc across last 12 sts. Ch 1, turn. **Row 4:** With MC, [sc in next st, dc in next st] 6 times, with CC, hdc in last 2 sts. Ch 2, turn. **Row 5:** With CC, hdc in first 2 sts, with MC, [sc in next st, dc in next st] 6 times. Ch 1, turn. Rep rows 4 and 5 for pat st and front band and work even until piece measures 1¾" from beg, end on WS.

Armhole

Next Row (RS): Work across first 11 sts. Ch 3, turn. Keeping to pat st (as described in Note 3) and front band as established, work even until piece measures 2¾" from beg, end on WS. Fasten off both MC and CC. Turn ready for a RS row.

materials

Yarn
Richesse et Soie (25g/approx 145yd) by K1C2, 1 ball each #9243 Soft Sunrise (MC) and #9900 Jet (CC).

Crochet Hook
Size C (2) or size to obtain gauge.

Notions
Tapestry needle.
Large-eye sewing needle.
Small safety pin.
8 (4mm) gold pearls.
1 small metal snap.
6¾"-length of 2.25mm gold curb style chain.

notes

1. When changing color when working in sc, draw new color though 2 lps on hook to complete sc.
2. When changing color when working in hdc, draw new color though 3 lps on hook to complete hdc.
3. To keep to pat st when working shaping and dec, work as follows: always work a sc over a dc and a dc over a sc. When you end with a sc, ch 3 to turn. When you end with a dc, ch 1 to turn.

gauge

8 sts and 7 rows = 1" (in pat st).
FOR PROPER FIT, TAKE THE TIME TO CHECK YOUR GAUGE.

Classic Suit Ensemble

Work in a richly textured moss-stitch pattern using an exquisite silk and cashmere blend yarn in sugary-pink and bold black. A fabulously striking designer look any cover girl will love.

Shape Neck

Next Row (RS): Sk first 5 sts, join MC with a dc in next st, work across last 5 sts—6 sts. Keeping to pat st, dec 1 st at neck edge on next row, then every row once more—4 sts. Work even until front measures same length as back. Fasten off.

SLEEVES

Sew shoulder seams. From RS with MC, work 22 sc evenly spaced along armhole edge. Ch 1, turn. **Row 1:** * Sc in next st, dc in next st, rep from * across. Ch 1, turn. Rep this row for pat st and work even for ½", end on WS. Keeping to pat st, dec 1 st each side of next row, then every 4th row twice more—16 sts. Work even until sleeve measures 2⅝" from beg, end on RS. **Next Row:** Sc in each st across. Change to CC, ch 1, turn. **Next 2 Rows:** Sc in each st across. After last row is completed, fasten off.

FINISHING

Neck Edging

Row 1: From RS, sk first 2 CC sts of right front, join MC with a sc in next st. Making sure that work lies flat, work 23 more sc evenly spaced along neck edge to within last 2 CC sts of left front—24 sts. Fasten off. **Row 2:** From RS, join CC in first st of right front neck edge with a sc. Sc in each st across entire neck edge. Ch 1, turn. **Row 3:** Sc in each st across. Fasten off.

Mock Pocket Flaps
(make 2)

Leaving a long end for sewing, with CC, ch 6. **Row 1:** Sc in 2nd ch from hook and in each ch across—5 sts.

Fasten off leaving a long end. With bottom lps of beg ch at top, sew each flap to front so bottom edge is ½" from bottom edge of jacket and side edge of flap is ½" from front edge.

Sew sleeve and side seams. On left front, sew on 5 pearl buttons, with the first ¼" from top edge, the last ¼" from bottom edge and 3 spaced evenly between. Sew a button to center bottom of each pocket flap. To close jacket, push beads between sts.

skirt

Skirt is made in one piece. Beg at bottom edge, with CC, ch 43. **Row 1 (RS):** Sc in 2nd ch from hook and in each ch across—42 sts. Ch 1, turn. **Row 2:** Sc in each st across. Change to MC, ch 1, turn. **Row 3:** Rep row 2. Ch 1, turn. **Pattern St—Row 1:** * Sc in next st, dc in next st, rep from * across. Ch 1, turn. Rep this row until piece measures 2⅞" from beg, end on WS. Ch 1, turn.

Shape Waist

Dec Row 1 (RS): Sc in first 2 sts, * dec 1 st over next 2 sts, sc in next 4 sts, rep from * across, end last rep sc in last 2 sts—35 sts. Ch 1, turn. **Dec Row 2:** Sc in first st, * dec 1 st over next 2 sts, sc in next 3 sts, rep from * across, end last rep sc in last 2 sts—28 sts. Ch 1, turn. **Last Row:** Sc in each st across. Fasten off.

FINISHING

Sew back seam to within 1" of top edge. Sew snap to waist opening.

pillbox hat

With MC, ch 3. Join ch with a sl st forming a ring. **Rnd 1:** Work 6 sc over ch. Mark last st made with the safety pin. You will be working in a spiral marking the last st made with the safety pin to indicate end of rnd. **Rnd 2:** Work 2 sc in each st around—12 sts. **Rnd 3:** * Sc in next st, work 2 sc in next st, rep from * around—18 sts. **Rnd 4:** * Sc in next 2 sts, work 2 sc in next st, rep from * around—24 sts. **Rnd 5:** * Sc in next 3 sts, work 2 sc in next st, rep from * around—30 sts. **Rnd 6:** * Sc in next 4 sts, work 2 sc in next st, rep from * around—36 sts. Ch 1, turn. **Pattern St—Row 1:** * Sc in next st, dc in next st, rep from * across. Rep this row for ½", end on RS. Ch 1, turn. **Next Row:** Sc in each st across. Change to CC, ch 1, turn. **Next 2 Rows:** Sc in each st across. Ch 1, turn. After last row is completed, fasten off.

FINISHING
Sew back seam.
Top Loop
With CC, tightly ch 7. Fasten off. Sew to center top of hat.

shoulder bag

Made in one piece. Beg at base, with CC, ch 11. **Row 1:** Sc in 2nd ch from hook and in each ch across—10 sts. Ch 1, turn. **Rows 2 and 3:** Sc in each st across. Ch 1, turn. After row 3 is completed, ch 1, turn to side

edge. **Rnd 1:** Work 3 sc evenly spaced in side edge. Turn to bottom lps of beg ch and work 1 sc in each of 10 lps. Turn to next side edge and work 3 sc evenly spaced. Turn to top edge and work 1 sc in each of 10 sts—26 sts. Work 7 more rnds, end in center of one long side. Fasten off.
Flap
On opposite side, locate 10 center sts. **Row 1:** Join yarn with a sc in first st, ch 1, sk next st, sc in next 6 sts, ch 1, sk next st, sc in last st. Ch 1, turn. **Row 2:** Sc in each st and over each ch-1 sp across. Ch 1, turn. **Row 3:** Sc in first st, ch 1, sk next st, sc in next 6 sts, ch 1, sk next st, sc in last st. Ch 1, turn. **Row 4:** Rep row 2. Ch 1, turn. **Rows 5–7:** Sc in each st across. Ch 1, turn. **Row 8:** Dec 1 st over firsts 2 sts, sc in next 2 sts, ch 2, sk next 2 sts, sc in next 2 sts, dec 1 st over last 2 sts—8 sts. Ch 1, turn. **Row 9:** Dec 1 st over first 2 sts, sc in next st, work 2 sc over ch-2 sp, sc in next st, dec 1 st over last 2 sts—6 sts. Fasten off.

FINISHING
Using sewing needle, weave CC through gold chain leaving long yarn ends. Fasten yarn securely to each end of gold chain. Working through ch-1 sps on flap, weave gold chain though flap, as shown. Sew ends of gold chain together on inside of flap. Sew pearl button to front of bag to correspond to ch-2 sp on flap.

Five Easy Pieces

These basic mix-and-match pieces create a designer-look wardrobe that fits in one suitcase...just perfect for a high-profile jet-setter. Jacket, skirt, pants, camisole and shoulder bag are all worked in single crochet. They make the perfect essentials for the next Barbie® adventure.

jacket

BACK

Beg at bottom edge, with larger hook and A, ch 20. **Row 1 (WS):** Sc in 2nd ch from hook and in each ch across—19 sts. Ch 1, turn. **Row 2:** Sc in each st across. Ch 1, turn. Rep row 2 for pat st and work even until piece measures 3¼" from beg, end on WS.

Right Shoulder

Work across first 6 sts, ch 1, turn. Work even for 1 row. Fasten off.

Left Shoulder

From RS, sk center 7 sts (neck edge), join yarn with a sc in next st, work across last 5 sts. Ch 1, turn. Work even for 1 row. Fasten off.

LEFT FRONT

With larger hook and A, ch 14. **Row 1 (WS):** Sc in 2nd ch from hook and in each ch across—13 sts. Ch 1, turn. **Row 2:** Sc in each st across. Ch 1, turn. Rep row 2 for pat st and work even until piece measures 2⅞" from beg, end on WS.

Shape Neck

Work across first 9 sts, ch 1, turn. Dec 1 st at neck edge every row 3 times—6 sts. Work even until piece measures 3½" from beg. Fasten off.

RIGHT FRONT

Work same as for left front until piece measures 2⅞" from beg, end on WS. Do not ch, turn.

Shape Neck
Sl st across first 4 sts, ch 1, work across last 9 sts, ch 1, turn. Dec 1 st at neck edge every row 3 times—6 sts. Work even until piece measures 3½" from beg. Fasten off.

SLEEVES
Lightly steam-press all pieces. Sew shoulder seams. Measure and mark 1¼" from shoulder seam on fronts and back. From RS, join yarn with a sc at marker using larger hook. Work 20 more sc evenly spaced across armhole edge to next marker—21 sts. Ch 1, turn. Work even in sc for 1". Dec 1 st each side on next row, then every 4th row twice more—15 sts. Work even until sleeve measures 3" from beg. Fasten off.

FINISHING
Collar
From RS with larger hook and A, join yarn with a sc after last sl st of right front neck shaping. Work 28 more sc evenly spaced across neck edge to left neck shaping—29 sts. Ch 1, turn. Work even in sc for 5 more rows. Fasten off. Sew side edges of collar to top of front necks.
Lightly steam-press jacket. Sew side and sleeve seams.
Front Edging
From RS with larger hook and A, join yarn with a sc in first row of left front edge. Working from left to right, sc evenly around entire edge making sure that work lies flat.
On left front, sew first pearl button just below beg of neck shaping, then 2 more below it, spacing them ½" apart. To close jacket, push beads between sts.

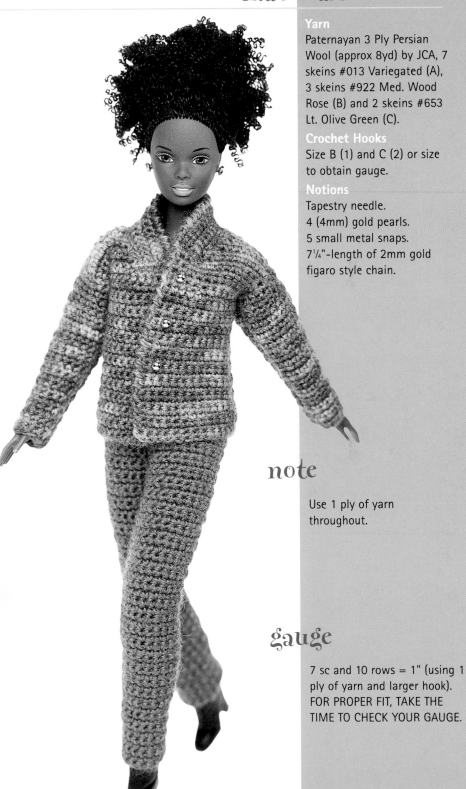

Yarn
Paternayan 3 Ply Persian Wool (approx 8yd) by JCA, 7 skeins #013 Variegated (A), 3 skeins #922 Med. Wood Rose (B) and 2 skeins #653 Lt. Olive Green (C).
Crochet Hooks
Size B (1) and C (2) or size to obtain gauge.
Notions
Tapestry needle.
4 (4mm) gold pearls.
5 small metal snaps.
7¼"-length of 2mm gold figaro style chain.

note

Use 1 ply of yarn throughout.

gauge

7 sc and 10 rows = 1" (using 1 ply of yarn and larger hook). FOR PROPER FIT, TAKE THE TIME TO CHECK YOUR GAUGE.

Five Easy Pieces

Make the buttoned jacket in a richly colored variegated yarn, then make the other separates using colors that match it perfectly. To extend the wardrobe even more, make more pieces in other matching colors.

skirt

Made in one piece. Beg at bottom edge, with larger hook and A, ch 39.
Row 1 (WS): Sc in 2nd ch from hook and in each ch across—38 sts. Ch 1, turn. **Row 2:** Sc in each st across. Ch 1, turn. Rep row 2 for pat st and work even until piece measures 2½" from beg.
Shape Waist
Dec Row 1: Sc in first 3 sts, * dec 1 st over next 2 sts, sc in next 4 sts, rep from * across, end last rep sc in last 3 sts—32 sts. Ch 1, turn. Work even for 1 row. **Dec Row 2:** Sc in first 4 sts, * dec 1 st over next 2 sts, sc in next 3 sts, rep from * across—26 sts. Ch 1, turn. Work even for 3 rows. Fasten off.

FINISHING
Lightly steam-press skirt. Beg ½" from bottom edge, sew back seam to within 1" of top edge. Sew a snap to waist opening.

pants

Make 2 pieces. Beg at bottom edge, with larger hook and B, ch 17. **Row 1:** Sc in 2nd ch from hook and in each ch across—16 sts. Ch 1, turn. **Row 2:** Sc in each st across. Ch 1, turn. Rep row 2 for pat st and work even until leg measures 1" from beg, end on WS.

SHAPE LEG
Inc 1 st each side of next row, then every 8th row 3 times more—24 sts. Work even until leg measures 5" from beg, end on WS. Do not ch, turn.
Shape Crotch
Sl st across first 2 sts, ch 1, work across to within last 2 sts—20 sts. Ch 1, turn. Work even for 1 row. Dec 1 st each side of next row—18 sts. Ch 1, turn. Work even until leg measures 6¼" from beg, end on WS.
Shape Waist
Dec Row: Sc in first 2 sts, * dec 1 st over next 2 sts, sc in next 2 sts, rep from * across—14 sts. Ch 1, turn. Change to smaller hook. Work even for 1 row. Fasten off.

FINISHING
Lightly steam-press pieces. Sew front seam. Sew back seam to within 1" of top edge. Sew leg seams. Sew a snap to waist opening.

camisole

Made in one piece. **Ribbing:** Worked vertically. With smaller hook and C, ch 5. **Row 1:** Sc in 2nd ch from hook and in each ch across—4 sts. Ch 1, turn. **Row 2:** Working through back lps only, sc in each st across. Ch 1, turn. Rep row 2 for pat st and work even until piece measures 3½" from beg. Change to larger hook. Ch 1, turn to long edge of ribbing. **Next Row (RS):** Work 39 sc evenly spaced across long edge of ribbing. Ch 1, turn. Work even in sc until piece measures 2½" from beg, end on WS. Fasten off.
Left Strap
From RS, sk first 13 sts, join C with a sc in next st using smaller hook, sc in next 2 sts—3 sts. Ch 1, turn. Work even in sc until strap measures 2" from beg. Fasten off.
Right Strap
From RS, sk next 7 sts, join C with a sc in next st using smaller hook, sc in next 2 sts—3 sts. Ch 1, turn. Continue to work same as for left strap.

FINISHING

Lightly steam-press piece, but do not press ribbing. For each strap, sew end to top back edge, positioning it so there are 7 underarm sts.

Back Edging

From RS with smaller hook and C, sc evenly across each back edge making sure that work lies flat. Fasten off. Sew 3 snaps evenly spaced along back opening.

shoulder bag

With larger hook and B, ch 11. **Row 1 (WS):** Sc in 2nd ch from hook and in each ch across—10 sts. Ch 1, turn. **Row 2:** Sc in each st across. Ch 1, turn. Rep row 2 for pat st and work even until piece measures 2" from beg, end on WS.

Flap

Dec 1 st each side on next row, then every other row 3 times more—2 sts. Fasten off.

FINISHING

Fold bottom of bag up to beg of flap decs; pin to secure. Turn over so back of bag is facing you. With smaller hook and A, and working through both thicknesses, sc first side of bag together. Making sure that work lies flat, sc evenly along entire flap edge, then sc opposite side of bag together. Fasten off. Sew on a gold pearl to correspond to center point of flap. Sew ends of gold chain in place. To close bag, push bead between sts.

Cozy Country Casuals

Barbie® doll's three-quarter-length anorak features a drawstring waist, hood and single-button closure at the neck. Single crocheted in one piece, it boasts ribbed cuffs and hem.

Ken® wears a sporty buffalo plaid jacket and dons a matching cap. And don't forget to make a spiffy tweed coat for the dog. It features a wide ribbed collar.

anorak

BODY

Made in one piece. **Ribbing:** Ribbing is made vertically. With smaller hook and A, ch 5. **Row 1:** Sc in 2nd ch from hook and in each ch across—4 sts. Ch 1, turn. **Row 2:** Working through back lps only, sc in each st across. Ch 1, turn. Rep row 2 for rib pat and work even until piece measures 5¾" from beg. Ch 1, turn to long edge of ribbing. **Foundation Row (RS):** Work 50 sc evenly spaced across long edge of ribbing. Change to larger hook, ch 1, turn. Work even in sc until piece measures 3" from beg, end on WS. Join B, ch 1, turn.

RIGHT FRONT

Work across first 14 sts. Ch 1, turn. Work even until piece measures 4⅜" from beg, end on WS. Do not ch, turn.

Shape Neck

Sl st across first 6 sts, work across last 7 sts—8 sts. Ch 1, turn. Dec 1 st at neck edge on next row, then every row twice more—5 sts. Work even until piece measures 4⅞" from beg, end on WS. Fasten off.

ANORAK
Yarn
Special Blauband (50g/210m/225yd) by Froehlich Wolle, 1 skein each #7107 Black/Burgundy Tweed (A) and #10 Black (B).
Crochet Hooks
Sizes B (1) and C (2) or size to obtain gauge.
Notions
Tapestry needle.
1 black 6/0 "E" bead.

note

When changing colors, draw new color through 2 lps on hook to complete sc.

gauge

7 sc and 9 rows = 1" (using larger hook).
FOR PROPER FIT, TAKE THE TIME TO CHECK YOUR GAUGE.

Cozy Country Casuals

Crochet these winning outdoor fashions using warm 'n woolly stocking-weight yarn. And if you make 'em all, you'll need just one skein of each yarn color.

BACK

From RS, sk next st, join B with a sc in next st, work across next 19 sts—20 sts. Ch 1, turn. Work even until back measures same length as right front, end on WS. Fasten off.

LEFT FRONT

From RS, sk next st, join B with a sc in next st, work across last 13 sts—14 sts. Ch 1, turn. Work even until piece measures 4³⁄₈" from beg, end on WS. Ch 1, turn.

Shape Neck

Work across first 8 sts. Ch 1, turn. Dec 1 st at neck edge on next row, then every row twice more—5 sts. Work even until piece measures 4⁷⁄₈" from beg, end on WS. Fasten off.

SLEEVES

Sew shoulder seams. From RS, with B, work 24 sc evenly spaced along armhole edge. Ch 1, turn. Work even in sc until sleeve measures 1" from beg, end on WS. Dec 1 st each side on next row, then every 4th row 3 times more—16 sts. Work even until sleeve measures 2⁷⁄₈" from beg, end on WS. Fasten off.

FINISHING

Hood

From RS, sk first 5 sts of right front. Join A with a sc in next st, then work 20 more sc evenly spaced along neck edge to within last 5 sts of left front—21 sts. Ch 1, turn. **Inc Row:** Sc in first st, [work 2 sc in next st, sc in next st] 10 times—31 sts. Work even until piece measures 2⁷⁄₈" from beg. Fasten off. Sew hood seam.

Cuffs

With smaller hook and B, ch 5. **Row 1:** Sc in 2nd ch from hook and in each ch across—4 sts. Ch 1, turn. **Row 2:** Working through back lps only, sc in each st across. Ch 1, turn. Rep row 2 for rib pat and work even until piece measures 2" from beg. Fasten off. Sew cuffs to bottom edge of sleeves, easing in fullness. Sew sleeve seams.

Drawstring

With smaller hook and A, tightly crochet a ch to measure 12". Fasten off leaving a long end. Thread end into needle. From RS, measure 2" from bottom edge of right front, then count 5 sts in from front edge. Weave drawstring along row, going under and over groups of 2 or 3 sts, exiting 5 sts from left front edge. Tightly knot each end of drawstring. Trim off excess yarn close to knots. On left front, sew bead just below first st of hood. To close anorak, push bead between sts.

buffalo plaid jacket

BODY

Made in one piece. **Ribbing:** Ribbing is made vertically. With smaller hook and A, ch 6. **Row 1:** Sc in 2nd ch from hook and in each ch across—5 sts. Ch 1, turn. **Row 2:** Working through back lps only, sc in each st across. Ch 1, turn. Rep row 2 for rib pat and work even until piece measures 5½" from beg. Ch 1, turn to long edge of ribbing. **Foundation Row (WS):** Work 49 sc evenly spaced across long edge of ribbing.

Chart

Change to larger hook, ch 2, turn. Work now in hdc, with a ch-2 turn at end of each row. Beg chart on row 1 (RS). Work from V to W (right front band). Rep from W to X 7 times, then end at Y. Work from Y to Z (left front band). Work even to row 4, then rep rows 1-4 once more, end on WS. Ch 2, turn.

Color Key

■ Black A

● Burgundy B

▨ Black/Burgundy Tweed C

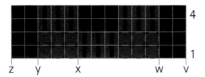

RIGHT FRONT

Keeping to charted design, work across first 11 sts. Ch 2, turn. Work even until 3 reps of rows 1-4 have been completed from beg; then work rows 1 and 2. Fasten off. Turn ready for a RS row.

Shape Neck

From RS, sk first 5 sts. Keeping to charted design as established, join color in progress with a sc in next st, then work across last 5 sts—6 sts. Work even for 3 more rows. Fasten off.

BACK

From RS, sk next 3 sts. Keeping to charted design as established, join color in progress with a sc in next st, then work across next 20 sts—21 sts. Work even until back measures same length as right front, end on WS. Fasten off.

LEFT FRONT

From RS, sk next 3 sts. Keeping to charted design as established, join color in progress with a sc in next st, then work across last 10 sts—11 sts. Work even until 3 reps of rows 1-4 have been completed from beg; then work rows 1 and 2. Ch 2, turn.

Shape Neck

Keeping to charted design as established, work across first 6 sts. Ch 2, turn. Work even for 3 more rows. Fasten off.

materials

BUFFALO PLAID

Yarn

Special Blauband (50g/210m/225yd) by Froehlich Wolle, 1 skein each #10 Black (A), #7 Burgundy (B) and #7107 Black/Burgundy Tweed (C).

Crochet Hooks

Sizes B (1) and C (2) or size to obtain gauge.

Notions

Tapestry needle.
5 red Barbie buttons #47377 by JHB International.
5 small metal snaps.
1 small safety pin.

notes

1. When changing color, draw new color through 3 lps on hook to complete hdc.
2. Use a separate 36"-long strand of A for each front band.
3. Work hdc sts over color that's being carried across WS of work to prevent loose strands. Make sure to maintain gauge.
4. Carry colors from row to row, loosely along WS of work. Cut and join colors when necessary.

gauge

15 hdc and 10 rows = 2" (using larger hook).
FOR PROPER FIT, TAKE THE TIME TO CHECK YOUR GAUGE.

You can use leftover yarn to make more dog coats in solid colors.

SLEEVES

Ribbing: Work same as for body until piece measures 2¼" from beg. Ch 1, turn to long edge of ribbing.
Foundation Row (WS): Work 15 sc evenly spaced across long edge of ribbing.
Chart
Change to larger hook. Join next color, ch 2, turn. Work now in hdc, with a ch-2 turn at end of each row. Beg chart on row 3 (RS). Work from W to X twice, then end at Y. Working inc into charted pat, inc 1 st each side on next row, then every other row 6 times more—29 sts. Work even until a total of 16 charted rows have been completed, end on WS. Fasten off.

FINISHING

Draw in all loose ends. Sew shoulder seams.
Collar
Ribbing: With larger hook and A, ch 11. **Row 1:** Sc in 2nd ch from hook and in each ch across—10 sts. Ch 1, turn. **Row 2:** Working through back lps only, sc in each st across. Ch 1, turn. Rep row 2 for rib pat and work even until piece measures 4¾" from beg. Fasten off.
Beg 2 sts from front edge, sew one long edge of collar to neck edge, ending 2 sts from opposite front edge. Fold collar over to WS and sew in place. Sew sleeve seams. Sew in sleeves. Turn up cuffs. On left

front band, sew on buttons with the first ⅛" from top edge, the last ¼" from bottom edge and 3 spaced evenly between. Sew on snaps (positioning them same as buttons), along front bands so left front band overlaps right front band.

hat

With larger hook and C, ch 3. Join ch with a sl st forming a ring. **Rnd 1:** Work 6 sc over ch. Mark last st made with the safety pin. You will be working in a spiral marking the last st made with the safety pin to indicate end of rnd. **Rnd 2:** Work 2 sc in each st around—12 sts. **Rnd 3:** * Sc in next st, work 2 sc in next st, rep from * around—18 sts. **Rnd 4:** * Sc in next 2 sts, work 2 sc in next st, rep from * around—24 sts. **Rnd 5:** * Sc in next 3 sts, work 2 sc in next st, rep from * around—30 sts. **Rnd 6:** * Sc in next 4 sts, work 2 sc in next st, rep from * around—36 sts. **Rnd 7:** Working through back lps only, sc in each st around. Work now through both lps. **Rnds 8–12:** Sc in each st around. After rnd 12 is completed, join rnd with a sl st in next st (center back of hat). Fasten off.

DOG COAT
Yarn
Special Blauband
(50g/210m/225yd) by
Froehlich Wolle, 1 skein
#7107 Black/Burgundy
Tweed.
Crochet Hooks
Size B (1) and C (2) or size
to obtain gauge.
Notions
Tapestry needle.
1 small metal snap.

FINISHING

Visor

From RS, count 12 sts from center back of hat. With larger hook, join A with a sc in next st, sc in next 12 sts—13 sts. Ch 1, turn. Working in sc, dec 1 st each side on next row, then every row 3 times more—5 sts. Fasten off.

Left Ear Flap

From RS, sk 1 st from last st of visor. With larger hook, join A with a sc in next st, sc in next 4 sts—5 sts. Ch 1, turn. Work even in sc for 3 rows. **Dec Row 1:** Dec 1 st over first 2 sts, sc in next st, dec 1 st over last 2 sts—3 sts. Ch 1, turn. **Dec Row 2:** Draw up a lp in each of next 3 sts, yo and draw though all lps on hook—1 st. Change to smaller hook. **Tie:** Ch 25. Fasten off.

Right Ear Flap

From RS, count 6 sts from first st of visor. With larger hook, join A with a sc in 6th st, sc in next 4 sts— 5 sts. Cont to work same as for left ear flap.

dog coat

Made in one piece. **Collar:** Ribbing is made vertically. With smaller hook, ch 5. **Row 1:** Sc in 2nd ch from hook and in each ch across—4 sts. Ch 1, turn. **Row 2:** Working through back lps only, sc in each st across. Ch 1, turn. Rep row 2 for rib pat and work even until piece measures 4" from beg. Ch 1, turn to long edge of ribbing. **Foundation Row:** Work 30 sc evenly spaced across long edge of ribbing. Change to larger hook, ch 2, turn. **Row 1:** Hdc in each st across. Ch 2, turn. Rep this row for pat st and work even for 1 more row.

Shape Sides

Dec 1 st each side on next row, then every other row twice more—24 sts. Work even for 2 rows. Dec 1 st each side on next row, then every row 5 times more—12 sts. Fasten off.

FINISHING

Sew collar seam.

Strap

Work ribbing same as for collar until piece measures 1¾"-long. Fasten off. Sew one short edge of strap to center of left side edge of coat. Sew snap to opposite short edge of strap and to right side of coat, so that strap fastens on WS.

gauge

15 hdc and 10 rows = 2"
(using larger hook).
FOR PROPER FIT, TAKE THE
TIME TO CHECK YOUR GAUGE.

Sunday in the Park

In the park or around the town, Ken® and Barbie® make stylish statements in their casual fashions. The basketweave pullover features ribbed turtle-neck, cuffs and hem. The playful poncho boasts a four-color stripe repeat and is worked from the neck down. Increases at the front and back create the points.

basketweave pullover

STITCH GLOSSARY

FRDC (front raised dc)
Yo. Working from front to back to front, insert hook around post of st of row below. Yo, draw up a lp, [yo and draw through 2 lps on hook] twice.

BRDC (back raised dc)
Yo. Working from back to front to back, insert hook around post of st of row below. Yo, draw up a lp, [yo and draw through 2 lps on hook] twice.

BACK

Ribbing: Ribbing is made vertically. With smaller hook, ch 6. **Row 1:** Sc in 2nd ch from hook and in each ch across—5 sts. Ch 1, turn. **Row 2:** Working through back lps only, sc in each st across. Ch 1, turn. Rep row 2 for rib pat and work even until piece measures 3" from beg. Ch 1, turn to long edge of ribbing. **Foundation Row (RS):** Work 26 sc evenly spaced across long edge of ribbing. Change to larger hook. Ch 3, turn. **Next Row:** Dc in each st across. Ch 2, turn.

Basketweave Pattern
Row 1 (RS): Hdc in first st (selvage st), * FRDC around next 2 sts, BRDC around next 2 sts, rep from * across, end hdc in last st (selvage st). Ch 2, turn. **Row 2:** Hdc in first st, * BRDC around next 2 sts, FRDC around next 2 sts, rep from * across, end hdc in last st. Ch 2, turn. Rep these 2 rows for pat st. Work even until piece measures 2³⁄₄" from beg. Do not ch, turn.

Armholes
Sl st across first 4 sts, ch 2, hdc in next st, work in pat as established to within last 5 sts, end hdc in next st—18 sts. Ch 2, turn. Work even until piece measures 4" from beg. Fasten off.

FRONT

Work same as for back until piece measures 3³⁄₈" from beg.

Front Neck
First Side—Next Row: Hdc in first st, work in pat st across next 4 sts, hdc in next st. Ch 2, turn. Work even until front measures same length as back. Fasten off. **Second Side—Next Row:** Sk 6 center sts, join yarn with a sl st in next st, ch 2 (counts as hdc selvage st), work in pat st across last 5 sts. Ch 2, turn. Work even until front measures same length as back. Fasten off.

SLEEVES

Ribbing: Work same as for back until piece measures 2" from beg. Ch 1, turn to long edge of ribbing. **Foundation Row (RS):** Work 18 sc evenly spaced across long edge of ribbing. Change to larger hook. Ch 3, turn. **Next Row:** Dc in each st across. Ch 2, turn. Work even in pat st same as for back until sleeve measures 1¹⁄₂" from beg. **Inc Row:**

BASKETWEAVE PULLOVER
Yarn
True 4ply Botany (50g/170m) by Rowan, 1 ball #571 Lavender.
Crochet Hooks
Sizes B (1) and C (2) or size to obtain gauge.
Notions
Tapestry needle.

GRANNY STRIPE PONCHO
Yarn
Medicis Tapestry Wool (27.3yd/25m) by DMC, 2 skeins Ecru (MC) and 1 skein each #8426 Med. Blue Green (A), #8209 Very Lt. Colonial Blue (B) and #8223 Med. Shell Pink (C).
Crochet Hook
Steel crochet hook size 8 or size to obtain gauge.
Notions
Tapestry needle.

gauges

PULLOVER
14 sts and 9 rows = 2" (in pat st using larger hook).
PONCHO
24 dc with 7 ch-1 sps and 13 rnds = 2" (in pat st).
FOR PROPER FIT, TAKE THE TIME TO CHECK YOUR GAUGE.

Sunday in the Park

Work 2 hdc in first st, work across to last st, work 2 hdc in last st—20 sts. Ch 2, turn. **Following Row:** Keeping 1 hdc each side for selvage sts, work new sts into pat st. Work even until sleeve measures 2¼" from beg. Rep inc row and following row—22 sts. Work even until sleeve measures 3½" from beg. Fasten off.

FINISHING
Sew shoulder seams.
Turtleneck
With smaller hook, ch 12. Work in ribbing same as for back until piece measures 3" from beg. Fasten off. Sew short edges together. Sew turtleneck to neck edge, centering seam at center back neck edge. Sew on sleeves. Sew side and sleeve seams.

granny stripe poncho

Poncho is made in one piece from the top down. With MC, ch 54. Join ch with a sl st forming a ring. **Rnd 1 (RS):** Beg at back, ch 3 (always counts as 1 dc), work 2 dc over ring, [ch 1, work 3 dc over ring] 8 times, ch 1, (3 dc, ch 2, 3 dc) over ring, [ch 1, work 3 dc over ring] 8 times, ch 1, work 3 dc over ring, ch 2. Join rnd with a sl st in 3rd ch of ch-3. Fasten off. Join A with a sl st in back ch-2 sp.

Rnd 2 (RS): Ch 3, work 2 dc in same ch-2 sp, [ch 1, work 3 dc in next ch-1 sp] 9 times, ch 1, (work 3 dc, ch 2, 3 dc) in front ch-2 sp, [ch 1, work 3 dc in next ch-1 sp] 9 times, ch 1, work 3 dc in back ch-2 sp, ch 2. Join rnd with a sl st in 3rd ch of ch-3. Fasten off. Join MC with a sl st in back ch-2 sp.

Rnd 3 (RS): Ch 3, work 2 dc in same ch-2 sp, [ch 1, work 3 dc in next ch-1 sp] 10 times, ch 1, (work 3 dc, ch 2, 3 dc) in front ch-2 sp, [ch 1, work 3 dc in next ch-1 sp] 10 times, ch 1, work 3 dc in back ch-2 sp, ch 2. Join rnd with a sl st in 3rd ch of ch-3. Fasten off. Join B with a sl st in back ch-2 sp.

Rnd 4 (RS): Ch 3, work 2 dc in same ch-2 sp, [ch 1, work 3 dc in next ch-1 sp] 11 times, ch 1, (work 3 dc, ch 2, 3 dc) in front ch-2 sp, [ch 1, work 3 dc in next ch-1 sp] 11 times, ch 1, work 3 dc in back ch-2 sp, ch 2. Join rnd with a sl st in 3rd ch of ch-3. Fasten off. Join MC with a sl st in back ch-2 sp.

Rnd 5 (RS): Ch 3, work 2 dc in same ch-2 sp, [ch 1, work 3 dc in next ch-1 sp] 12 times, ch 1, (work 3 dc, ch 2, 3 dc) in front ch-2 sp, [ch 1, work 3 dc in next ch-1 sp] 12 times, ch 1, work 3 dc in back ch-2 sp, ch 2. Join rnd with a sl st in 3rd ch of ch-3. Fasten off. Join C with a sl st in back ch-2 sp.

Rnd 6 (RS): Ch 3, work 2 dc in same ch-2 sp, [ch 1, work 3 dc in next ch-1 sp] 13 times, ch 1, (work 3 dc, ch 2, 3 dc) in front ch-2 sp, [ch 1, work 3 dc in next ch-1 sp] 13 times, ch 1, work 3 dc in back ch-2 sp, ch 2. Join rnd with a sl st in 3rd

ch of ch-3. Fasten off. Join MC with
a sl st in back ch-2 sp. Cont to work
in pat st and stripe pat as established. Work until 10 MC rnds have
been completed. Fasten off.

FINISHING
Draw in all loose ends. Using a damp
pressing cloth, lightly steam-press so
that back and front bottom points
line up at center.

Symphony of Color

Whether window-shopping, lounging in a French café or driving in the country, Barbie® makes a winning statement wearing this colorful ensemble. Both the crewneck pullover and skirt feature flirty side slits. Make them in a richly textured moss-stitch pattern using a bold palette of wool yarn.

pullover

FRONT

Beg at bottom edge, with B, ch 23.

Row 1 (RS): Sc in 2nd ch from hook and in each ch across—22 sts. Ch 1, turn. **Row 2:** * Sc in next st, dc in next st, rep from * across. Ch 1, turn. Rep row 2 for pat st and work even for 1 more row. Join A, ch 1, turn.

Stripe Pattern

Working in pat st, work 3 rows A, 3 rows C and 3 rows B. Work even until 2 A stripes have been completed. Join C, do not ch, turn.

Armholes

Sl st across first 2 sts, ch 1, work across to within last 2 sts—18 sts. Ch 1, turn. Work even until 3 B stripes have been completed. Join A, ch 1, turn.

Shape Neck

First Side: Work across first 6 sts, ch 1, turn. Keeping to pat st, dec 1 st at neck edge every row twice—4 sts. Fasten off. **Second Side:** Sk 6 center sts, join A with a sc in next st, work across last 5 sts—6 sts. Ch 1, turn. Keeping to pat st, dec 1 st at neck edge every row twice—4 sts. Fasten off.

BACK

Work same as for front until arm-holes have been competed and 2 C stripes have been completed. Join B, ch 1, turn.

Divide for Back Opening

First Side: Work across first 9 sts, ch 3, turn. Keep to pat st as follows: always work a sc over a dc and a dc over a sc. When you end with a sc, ch 3 to turn. When you end with a dc, ch 1 to turn. Work even until piece measures same length as front to shoulders. Fasten off. **Second Side:** Join B with a dc in next st, keeping to pat st, work across last 8 sts—9 sts. Ch 1, turn. Cont to work same as for first side.

SLEEVES

Beg at bottom edge, with B, ch 13. **Row 1 (RS):** Sc in 2nd ch from hook and in each ch across—12 sts. Ch 1, turn. **Row 2:** * Sc in next st, dc in next st, rep from * across. Ch 1, turn. Rep row 2 for pat st and work even for 1 more row. Join A, ch 1, turn. Work in pat st and stripe pat same as for front, AT THE SAME TIME, keeping to pat st same as for back, inc 1 st each side on next row, then every 3rd row 3 times more—20 sts. Work even until 2 C stripes have been completed. Fasten off.

FINISHING

Sew shoulder seams.

Neck Edging

From RS with A, work 22 sc evenly spaced along entire neck edge. Ch 1, turn. Work even in sc for 2 more rows. Fasten off.

Sew on sleeves. Lightly steam-press piece. Beg 2 stripes from bottom edge, sew side seams. Sew sleeve seams. Sew snap to top of back neck opening.

skirt

Bottom of skirt is made in 3 panels to form side slits, then pieces are joined tog.

Center Front Panel

Beg at bottom edge, with A , ch 19. **Row 1 (RS):** Sc in 2nd ch from hook and in each ch across—18 sts. Ch 1, turn. **Row 2:** * Sc in next st, dc in next st, rep from * across. Ch 1, turn. Rep row 2 for pat st and work even for 4 more rows, end on WS. Fasten off; set aside.

Right Back Panel

Beg at bottom edge, with A , ch 11. **Row 1 (RS):** Sc in 2nd ch from hook and in each ch across—10 sts. Ch 1, turn. **Row 2:** * Sc in next st, dc in next st, rep from * across. Ch 1, turn. Rep row 2 for pat st and work even for 4 more rows, end on WS. Fasten off; set aside.

Left Back Panel

Work same as for right back panel. Do not fasten off.

Join Panels

Next Row (RS): Keeping to pat st, work across 10 sts of left back panel, 18 sts of center front panel and 10 sts of right back panel—38 sts. Ch 1, turn. Work even in pat st until piece measures 2¾" from beg, end on WS. Ch 1, turn.

Shape Waist

Dec Row 1: Sc in first 2 sts, [dec 1 st over next 2 sts, sc in next 2 sts] 9 times—29 sts. **Following Row:** Sc in each st across. Ch 1, turn. **Dec Row 2:** Sc in first 4 sts, [dec 1 st over next 2 sts, sc in next 2 sts] 6 times, end sc in last st—23 sts. Ch 1, turn. **Following Row:** Sc in each st across. Fasten off.

FINISHING

Lightly steam-press skirt. Sew back seam to within 1" of top edge. Sew a snap to waist opening.

materials

Yarn

Paternayan 3 Ply Persian Wool (approx 8yd) by JCA, 4 skeins #332 Lavender (A), and 2 skeins each #352 Magenta (B) and #545 Lt. Blue (C).

Crochet Hook

Size C (2) or size to obtain gauge.

Notions

Tapestry needle.
2 small metal snaps.

notes

1. Use 1 ply of yarn through-out.
2. When changing colors, draw new color through 2 lps on hook to complete sc.

gauge

15 sc and 12 rows = 2" (using 1 ply of yarn).
FOR PROPER FIT, TAKE THE TIME TO CHECK YOUR GAUGE.

Country Squire

A handsome tweed cardigan exudes casual elegance. Worked in quick and easy moss stitch, this enduring classic features a wide shawl collar and patch pockets.

Yarn
Rowanspun 4ply (25g/162yd)
by Rowan, 1 hank #701
Swarm.
Crochet Hooks
Sizes B (1) and C (2) or size to
obtain gauge.
Notions
Tapestry needle.
4 brown 6/0 "E" beads.

shawl collar cardigan

BACK

With larger hook, ch 25. **Row 1 (WS):** Sc in 2nd ch from hook and in each ch across—24 sts. Ch 1, turn. **Row 2:** * Sc in next st, dc in next st, rep from * across. Ch 1, turn. Rep row 2 for pat st and work even until piece measures 3¼" from beg, end on WS. Do not ch, turn.

Armholes

Sl st across first 3 sts, ch 3, work across to within last 3 sts—18 sts. Ch 3, turn. To establish pat st work as follows—**Next Row:** * Dc in next st, sc in next st, rep from * across. Ch 3, turn. Rep this row until piece measures 4¾" from beg. Fasten off.

LEFT FRONT

With larger hook, ch 13. **Row 1 (WS):** Sc in 2nd ch from hook and in each ch across—12 sts. Ch 1, turn. **Row 2:** * Sc in next st, dc in next st, rep from * across. Ch 1, turn. Rep row 2 for pat st and work even until piece measures 3¼" from beg, end on WS. Do not ch, turn.

Armhole

Sl st across first 3 sts, ch 3, finish row—9 sts. Ch 3, turn ready for a WS row.

Neck Shaping

Dec 1 st at beg of next row (neck edge), then at same edge every other row 4 times more—4 sts. AT THE SAME TIME, keep to pat st as follows: always work a sc over a dc and a dc over a sc. When you end with a sc, ch 3 to turn. When you end with a dc, ch 1 to turn. Work even until piece measures same length as back. Fasten off.

RIGHT FRONT

Work same as for left front until piece measures 3¼" from beg, end on WS. Ch 1, turn.

Armhole

Work across to within last 3 sts—9 sts. Ch 3, turn ready for a WS row.

Neck Shaping

Keeping to pat st, dec 1 st at end of next row (neck edge), then at same edge every other row 4 times more—4 sts. Work even until piece measures same length as back. Fasten off.

gauge

7 sts = 1" (in pat st
using larger hook).
FOR PROPER FIT, TAKE THE
TIME TO CHECK YOUR GAUGE.

Country Squire

Make the sweater using a knubby, wool tweed yarn. Use "E" beads for buttons in a color that matches the yarn.

SLEEVES

Ribbing: Ribbing is made vertically. With smaller hook, ch 6. **Row 1:** Sc in 2nd ch from hook and in each ch across—5 sts. Ch 1, turn. **Row 2:** Working through back lps only, sc in each st across. Ch 1, turn. Rep row 2 for rib pat and work even until piece measures 2" from beg. Ch 1, turn to long edge of ribbing. **Row 1 (RS):** Work 14 sc evenly spaced across long edge of ribbing. Change to larger hook, ch 1, turn. **Row 2:** * Sc in next st, dc in next st, rep from * across. Ch 1, turn. Keeping to pat st (same as for fronts), inc 1 st each side on next row, then every 4th row 3 times more—22 sts. Work even until sleeve measures 3½" from beg. Fasten off.

FRONT BAND/SHAWL COLLAR

Make 2 halves. **Ribbing:** With smaller hook, ch 5. **Row 1:** Sc in 2nd ch from hook and in each ch across—4 sts. Ch 1, turn. **Row 2:** Working through back lps only, sc in each st across. Ch 1, turn. Rep row 2 for rib pat and work even until piece measures 3¼" from beg. Ch 1, turn.

Shape Collar

Inc 1 st at beg of next row, then at same edge every other row 5 times more—10 sts. Work even until piece measures 5⅞" from beg. Fasten off.

POCKETS

Make 2. Beg at bottom edge, with larger hook, ch 7. **Row 1:** Sc in 2nd ch from hook and in each ch across—6 sts. Ch 1, turn. **Rows 2-4:** * Sc in next st, dc in next st, rep from * across. Ch 1, turn. **Row 5:** Sc in each st across. Fasten off.

FINISHING

Sew shoulder seams. Sew shawl collar seam. Pin front band/shawl collar to front/neck edge, centering collar seam at center of back neck edge. Work each side separately. Beg at bottom edge, sew for 3¼", then reverse seam and cont along to center of back neck edge. Lightly steam-press seams. Fold over collar and lightly steam-press in place. Sew on sleeves. Sew side and sleeve seams. Sew on each pocket so that bottom edge is ⅜" from bottom edge of front and centered between side and front band seams.

On right front band, sew on 4 bead buttons, with the first ¼" from beg of shawl collar shaping, the last ¼" from bottom edge and 2 spaced evenly between. To close cardigan, push beads between sts.

Terrific Terry Robe

Pamper Barbie® with a plush terry robe, the ultimate gift in comfort. It's made in single crochet which stitches up in a jiffy when worked in "Fuzzy Stuff" yarn. The shawl collar is worked as the piece is made, while the sash and patch pocket are made separately. If you would like to make a full-length robe, you'll need four additional cards of yarn.

Yarn
Fuzzy Stuff (20yd) by
Rainbow Gallery, 7 cards
#F216 Wedgwood.
Crochet Hook
Size C (2) or size to obtain
gauge.
Notions
Tapestry needle.

robe

BACK
Beg at bottom edge, ch 22. **Row 1:** Sc in 2nd ch from hook and in each ch across—21 sts. Ch 1, turn. **Row 2:** Sc in each st across. Ch 1, turn. Rep row 2 for pat st and work even until piece measures 5" from beg. Fasten off.

LEFT FRONT
Beg at bottom edge, ch 16. **Row 1:** Sc in 2nd ch from hook and in each ch across—15 sts. Ch 1, turn. **Row 2:** Sc in each st across. Ch 1, turn. Rep row 2 for pat st and work even until piece measures 5" from beg.
Shawl Collar
Work across first 9 sts, ch 1, turn. Work even for ¾". Fasten off.

RIGHT FRONT
Work same as for left front.

SLEEVES
Sew shoulder seams. Measure and mark 1½" from shoulder seam on fronts and back. From RS, join yarn with a sc at marker. Work 24 more sc evenly spaced across armhole edge to next marker—25 sts. Ch 1, turn. Work even in sc for 1". Dec 1 st each side on next row, then every 4th row 4 times more—15 sts. Work even until sleeve measures 3½" from beg. Fasten off.

POCKET
Beg at bottom edge, ch 8. **Row 1:** Sc in 2nd ch from hook and in each ch across—7 sts. Ch 1, turn. Work even in sc until pocket measures ¾" from beg. Fasten off.

sash

Holding 2 strands of yarn together, make a ch to measure 11½". Fasten off.

FINISHING
With RS facing, sew shawl collar seam. Sew edge of collar to back neck edge. Sew side and sleeve seams. Turn back cuffs ½". Sew pocket to right front so bottom edge of pocket is ½" from bottom edge of robe and side edge of pocket is ½" from front edge of robe.

note

It's sometimes difficult seeing the sts when working with fuzzy yarn. For best results, count sts as you work across each row to make sure you do not skip or miss a st.

gauge

17 sc and 18 rows = 2".
FOR PROPER FIT, TAKE THE TIME TO CHECK YOUR GAUGE.

Santa Fe Style

What better jacket to wear when exploring the canyons than one in colors inspired by the majestic sunsets of the southwest. The fly front jacket is hip-length and features dropped-shoulder sleeves. Make it using a novel long-stitch pattern and 1-ply wool yarn.

southwest striped jacket

STITCH GLOSSARY

L st = Long st. To make a long st: insert hook between 2 sts of 1 row below. Yo and draw up a lp to same height as row you are working on. Yo and draw through 2 lps on hook.

BODY

Made in one piece. Beg at bottom edge, with A, ch 48.

Long Stitch Pattern

Row 1 (RS): Sc in 2nd ch from hook and in each ch across—47 sts. Ch 1, turn. Row 2: Sc in each st across. Join B, ch 1, turn. Row 3 (RS): Sc in first 3 sts, * L st over next st, sc in next 3 sts, rep from * across. Row 4: Sc in each st across. Join C, ch 1, turn. Row 5 (RS): Sc in first st, * L st over next st, sc in next 3 sts, rep from * across, end L st over next st, sc in last st. Row 6: Sc in each st across. Join D, ch 1, turn. Rep rows 3-6 for pat st and AT THE SAME TIME, work in the following Stripe Pattern: 2 rows D, 2 rows E, 2 rows A, 2 rows B and 2 rows C. Work even until piece measures 3" from beg, end on WS.

RIGHT FRONT

Keeping to pat st and stripe pat, work across first 13 sts. Ch 1, turn. Work even until right front measures 5" from beg, end on WS. Sl last 2 lps on hook before completing last sc onto safety pin.

BACK

From RS, join color in progress with a sc in next st. Keeping to pat st and stripe pat, work across next 20 sts—21 sts. Ch 1, turn. Work even until back measures 5" from beg, end on WS. Fasten off.

LEFT FRONT

From RS, join color in progress with a sc in next st. Keeping to pat st and stripe pat, work across last 12 sts—13 sts. Ch 1, turn. Work even until left front measures 5" from beg, end on WS. Fasten off.

SLEEVES

Beg at bottom edge with A, ch 16.

Long Stitch Pattern

Row 1 (RS): Sc in 2nd ch from hook and in each ch across—15 sts. Ch 1, turn. **Row 2:** Sc in each st across. Join B, ch 1, turn. Beg on row 3, work in pat st and stripe pat same as for body, AT THE SAME TIME, when 4 rows have been completed, inc 1 st each side on next row, then every 4th row 5 times more, working incs into pat st—27 sts. Work even until sleeve measures 3" from beg, end on WS. Fasten off.

FINISHING

Draw in all loose ends. Sew a 6-st shoulder seam each side.

Collar

From WS, sl last 2 sts of right front onto hook. Join next stripe color, ch 1, turn. Keeping to pat st and stripe pat as established, work across 7 sts of right front, 9 sts of back and 7 sts of left front—23 sts. Ch 1, turn. Work even until 4 stripes have been completed. Fasten off.

Sew sleeve seams. Sew in sleeves.

materials

Yarn

Paternayan 3 Ply Persian Wool (approx 8yd) by JCA, 2 skeins each #832 Orange (A), #431 Dk. Brown (B), #611 Dk. Green (C), #732 Camel (D) and #702 Dk. Gold (E).

Crochet Hook

Size C (2) or size to obtain gauge.

Notions

Tapestry needle.
1 small safety pin.

notes

1. Use 1 ply of yarn throughout.
2. When changing colors, draw new color through 2 lps on hook to complete sc.

gauge

15 sts and 22 rows = 2" (in pat st using 1 ply of yarn). FOR PROPER FIT, TAKE THE TIME TO CHECK YOUR GAUGE.

Classic Camel Coat

As tailored classics make a comeback, make sure Barbie® leads the way in this timeless wrap coat. The modified A-line silhouette is easy to make in single crochet using an ultra-soft silk and cashmere blend yarn. Mohair yarn gives the illusion of faux-fur which adds a cozy and sophisticated finish to collar and cuffs.

coat

BACK

With MC, ch 33. **Row 1 (WS):** Sc in 2nd ch from hook and in each ch across—32 sts. Ch 1, turn. **Row 2:** Sc in each st across. Ch 1, turn. Rep row 2 for pat st and work even until piece measures 1½" beg, end on WS.

Shape Sides

Dec 1 st each side on next row, then every 1" 3 times more—24 sts. Work even until piece measures 8" from beg, end on WS. Fasten off.

LEFT FRONT

With MC, ch 21. **Row 1 (WS):** Sc in 2nd ch from hook and in each ch across—20 sts. Ch 1, turn. **Row 2:** Sc in each st across. Ch 1, turn. Rep row 2 for pat st and work even until piece measures 1½" beg, end on WS.

Shape Side

Dec 1 st at beg of next row, then at same edge every 1" 3 times more—16 sts. Work even until piece measures 5½" from beg, end on WS.

Shape Neck

Next Row: Work across to within last 2 sts, dec 1 st over last 2 sts. **Following Row:** Work even across. Continue to dec 1 st at neck edge every other row 9 times more, end on WS—6 sts. Fasten off.

RIGHT FRONT

Work same as for left front, reversing side and neck shaping.

SLEEVES

Sew shoulder seams. From RS, measure and mark 1½" down from each shoulder seam on fronts and back. From RS, join MC with a sc at marker. Work 26 more sc evenly spaced across armhole edge to next marker—27 sts. Ch 1, turn. Working in sc, work even for 7 more rows, end on WS. Dec 1 st each side of next row, then every 4th row twice more—21 sts. Work even until sleeve

measures 2½" from beg, end on WS.

Fur Cuffs

Join 2 strands of CC, ch 1, turn. Working in sc, work even for 6 rows. Fasten off.

belt

Belt is made vertically. Beg at long side edge with MC, ch 91. **Row 1:** Sc in 2nd ch from hook and in each ch across—90 sts. Ch 1, turn. **Rows 2 and 3:** Sc in each st across. After row 3 is completed, fasten off.

FINISHING

Fur Collar

From RS, join MC in first row of right front. **Foundation Row:** Making sure work lies flat, sc evenly across entire front and back neck edges. Fasten off. On each front, place a safety pin marker at beg of neck shaping. Measure and place 2nd marker ½" from first, 3rd marker ½" from 2nd and 4th marker ½" from 3rd. **Row 1:** From RS, join 2 strands of CC with a sc at marker closest to right shoulder seam. Sc in each st to marker closest to left shoulder seam; remove these markers. Ch 1, turn. **Row 2:** Sc in each CC st across. Fasten off. **Row 3:** From RS, join CC with a sc at next marker closest to right shoulder seam. Sc in each MC and CC st to next marker closest to left shoulder seam; remove these markers. Ch 1, turn. **Row 4:** Sc in each CC st across. Fasten off. Rep rows 3 and 4 twice more. Fasten off. **Row 9:** From RS, join CC with a sc in first st of foundation row. Sc in each MC and CC st to last st of foundation row. Ch 1, turn. **Row 10:** Sc in each CC st across. Fasten off. Draw in all loose ends.

Sew side and sleeve seams. Turn back cuffs.

materials

Yarn

Richesse et Soie (25g/approx 145yd) by K1C2, 2 balls #9448 Butterscotch (MC) and Wisper (20yd) by Rainbow Gallery, 4 cards #W75 Brown (CC).

Crochet Hook

Size C (2) or size to obtain gauge.

Notions

Tapestry needle.
8 small safety pins.

notes

1. Use 2 strands of CC held together for fur trim.
2. When changing colors, draw new color through 2 lps on hook to complete sc.

gauge

8 sc and 10 rows = 1" (using MC).
FOR PROPER FIT, TAKE THE TIME TO CHECK YOUR GAUGE.

Winter's Eve

The graceful lines and simple silhouette of this stunning gown take refinement to a new level. The dress and matching shawl are both made in half-double crochet using a whisper-soft silk and cashmere blend yarn. Lusturous pearls add a dramatic touch to the edges of the shawl.

Yarn
Richesse et Soie (25g/approx 145yd) by K1C2, 1 ball #9146 Snow.
Crochet Hook
Size C (2) or size to obtain gauge.
Notions
Tapestry needle.
Beading needle.
Ecru beading thread.
29 (3mm) pearls.

gown

BACK

(make 2)
Beg at back center seam, ch 72.
Row 1: Hdc in 3rd ch from hook and in each ch across—70 sts. Ch 2, turn.
Rows 2-7: Hdc in each st across. Ch 2, turn.
Armhole
Row 8: Hdc across first 59 sts, do not work across last 11 sts. Ch 2, turn. **Row 9:** Hdc in each st across. Fasten off.

FRONT

Beg at side seam, ch 61. **Row 1:** Hdc in 3rd ch from hook and in each ch across—59 sts. Ch 2, turn.
Row 2: Hdc in each st across. Ch 13, turn.
Armhole
Row 3: Hdc in 3rd ch from hook and in next 10 ch, then hdc in each st across—70 sts. Ch 2, turn.
Rows 4-6: Hdc in each st across. Ch 2, turn. After row 6 is completed, do not ch, turn.
Front Neck
Row 7: Sl st across first 5 sts, ch 2, hdc in each st across—65 sts. Ch 2, turn. **Rows 8-12:** Hdc in each st across. Ch 2, turn. After row 12 is completed, ch 7 turn. **Row 13:** Hdc in 3rd ch from hook and in next 4 ch, then hdc in each st across—70 sts. Ch 2, turn. **Rows 14-16:** Hdc in each st across. Ch 2, turn. After row 16 is completed, do not ch, fasten off. Turn work.

Armhole

Row 17: Count 11 sts down from shoulder. Join yarn with a sl st in next st, ch 2, finish row—59 sts.
Row 18: Hdc in each st across. Fasten off.
Turtleneck
Beg at side edge, ch 12. **Row 1:** Hdc in 3rd ch from hook and in each ch across—10 sts. Ch 2, turn.
Row 2: Hdc in each st across. Ch 2, turn. Rep row 2 until piece measures 3¾" long. Fasten off.

FINISHING

Sew shoulder seams.
Armhole Edging
From RS, sc evenly along each armhole. Fasten off.
Sew turtleneck to neck edge. Sew back seam to within 2" of neck edge. Sew side seams. On right back, sew 1 pearl to neck edge, 1 pearl ½" above back seam and 3 evenly spaced between. On turtleneck, sew 1 pearl ⅛" from bottom edge and 1 pearl ¼" above it. To fasten closed, push pearls between sts.

shawl

Beg at long side edge, ch 90. **Row 1:** Hdc in 3rd ch from hook and in each ch across—88 sts. Ch 2, turn. **Row 2:** Hdc in each st across. Ch 2, turn. Rep row 2 until shawl measures 1¼" from beg. Fasten off.

FINISHING

Draw in all loose ends. Sew 11 pearls evenly spaced across each end.

note

All pieces are made vertically.

gauge

8 hdc and 6 rows = 1".
FOR PROPER FIT, TAKE THE TIME TO CHECK YOUR GAUGE.

Autumn Splendor

Fine lines, simple shaping and subtle textures make this figure-flattering outfit a fall favorite. The tweed mock turtleneck pullover is fashioned with a novel v-slit at the front and feminine bell-shaped sleeves. The coordinating, pumpkin-color wrap skirt features tweed stripes at the hem. Make them both in single crochet using woolly sport-weight yarns.

pullover

BACK

With A, ch 21. **Row 1 (WS):** Sc in 2nd ch from hook and in each ch across—20 sts. Ch 1, turn. **Row 2:** Sc in each st across. Ch 1, turn. Rep row 2 for pat st and work even until piece measures 1" from beg, end on WS. Ch 1, turn.

Shape Waist

Dec 1 st each side on next row, then every other row twice more, end on WS—14 sts. Ch 1, turn. Inc 1 st each side on next row, then every other row twice more—20 sts. Ch 1, turn. Work even until piece measures 2¾" from beg, end on WS. Do not ch, turn.

Armholes

Sl st across first 2 sts, ch 1, work across to within last 2 sts—16 sts. Ch 1, turn. Work even for 1 more row, end on WS.

Divide for Back Opening

Right Half—Next Row (RS): Work across first 8 sts, ch 1, turn. Work even until piece measures 4" from beg, end on WS. Fasten off. **Left Half—Next Row (RS):** Join yarn with a sc in next st, finish row—8 sts. Ch 1, turn. Cont to work same as for right half.

FRONT

V Shaping—Right Half: With A, ch 8. **Row 1:** Sc in 2nd ch from hook and in each ch across—7 sts. **Inc row (RS):** Working in sc, inc 1 st at beg of next row. Ch 1, turn. **Following Row:** Sc in each st across. Ch 1, turn. Rep these 2 rows twice more—10 sts. Fasten off; set aside.

Left Half

With A, ch 8. **Row 1:** Sc in 2nd ch from hook and in each ch across—7 sts. **Inc row (RS):** Working in sc, inc 1 st at end of next row. Ch 1, turn. **Following Row:** Sc in each st across. Ch 1, turn. Rep these 2 rows twice more—10 sts. Do not fasten off, ch 1, turn.

Join Fronts

Sc across 10 sts of left half, then 10 sts of right half—20 sts. Ch 1, turn. Work even for 1 more row. Beg at waist shaping, work same as for back (omitting back opening) until piece measures 4 rows less than back to shoulders, end on WS. Ch 1, turn.

Shape Neck

First Side—Next Row (RS): Sc across next 6 sts. Ch 1, turn. Dec 1 st at neck edge on next row, then every row once more—4 sts. Work even for 1 row. Fasten off. **Second Side—Next Row (RS):** Sk 4 center sts, join yarn with a sc in next st, finish row—6 sts. Ch 1, turn. Cont to work same as for first side.

SLEEVES

Sew shoulder seams. From RS, work 18 sc evenly spaced along armhole edge. Ch 1, turn. Work even for 5 more rows. Dec 1 st each side on next row, then every 4th row twice more—12 sts. Work even until sleeve measures 2¼" from beg, end on WS.

Bell Shaping

Inc 1 st each side on next row, then every 4th row once more—16 sts. Work even until sleeve measures 3" from beg, end on WS. Fasten off.

FINISHING

Lightly steam-press entire piece.

Mock Turtleneck

From RS, work 24 sc evenly spaced along entire neck edge. Ch 1, turn. Work even in sc for 3 more rows. Fasten off. Sew side and sleeve seams. Sew 1 snap to mock turtleneck.

wrap skirt

Made in one piece. With B, ch 47. **Row 1 (RS):** Sc in 2nd ch from hook and in each ch across—46 sts. Ch 1, turn. **Row 2:** Sc in each st across. Join A, ch 1, turn. **Rows 3 and 4:** Sc in each st across. Ch 1, turn. After row 4 is completed, join B, ch 1, turn. **Rows 5 and 6:** Sc in each st across. Ch 1, turn. After row 6 is completed, join A, ch 1, turn. **Row 7:** Sc in each st across. Join B, ch 1, turn. Work even in sc until piece measures 4¾" from beg, end on WS.

Shape Waist

Dec Row 1: Sc in first 4 sts, [dec 1 st over next 2 sts, sc in next 3 sts] 8 times, end sc in last 2 sts—38 sts. Ch 1, turn. **Following Row:** Sc in each st across. Ch 1, turn. **Dec Row 2:** Sc in first 3 sts, [dec 1 st over next 2 sts, sc in next 3 sts] 7 times—31 sts. Ch 1, turn. Work even for 2 more rows. Fasten off.

FINISHING

Steam-press piece. Overlap skirt at waist. Sew 2 snaps along waist to secure waist and overlap to underlap.

materials

Yarn
Rowanspun 4ply (25g/162yd) by Rowan, 1 hank #705 Spiced Orange (A) and True 4ply Botany (50g/170m) also by Rowan, 1 ball #583 Glow (B).

Crochet Hook
Size C (2) or size to obtain gauge.

Notions
Tapestry needle.
3 small metal snaps

note

When changing colors, draw new color through 2 lps on hook to complete sc.

gauge

15 sc and 18 rows = 2" (using A or B).
FOR PROPER FIT, TAKE THE TIME TO CHECK YOUR GAUGE.

Afternoon Tea

Afternoon tea never looked more fashionable. For a sleek look, a stunning teal sheath accented with bold black trim. A face-flattering hat dotted with richly textured cluster stitches completes the captivating outfit. For something demure, a dress featuring a fitted bodice, shoulder-hugging collar and a flirty, flared skirt. Pair the dress with a dramatic wide-brimmed picture hat.

stunning sheath dress

Made in one piece. Beg at bottom edge, with CC, ch 47. **Row 1 (RS):** Sc in 2nd ch from hook and in each ch across—46 sts. Ch 1, turn. **Row 2:** Sc in each st across. Join MC, ch 1, turn. **Row 3:** With MC, sc in first 11 sts, with CC, sc in next 2 sts, with MC, sc in next 20 sts, with CC, sc in next 2 sts, with MC, sc in last 11 sts. Ch 1, turn. Rep row 3 for pat st and color pat. Work even until piece measures 2¾" from beg, end on WS. Ch 1, turn.

Shape Waist
Keep to color pat as established. **Dec Row:** Sc in first 3 sts, [dec 1 st over next 2 sts, sc in next 2 sts] twice, work across next 5 sts, rep between [ ]'s 4 times, work across next 5 sts, [sc in next 2 sts, dec 1 st over next 2 sts] twice, sc in next 3 sts—38 sts. Work even until piece meaures 3⅜" from beg, end on WS. **Inc Row 1:** Sc in first 3 sts, [work 2 sc in next st, sc in next 2 sts] twice, work across next 5 sts, rep between [ ]'s 4 times, work across next 5 sts, [sc in next 2 sts, work 2 sc in next st] twice, sc in next 3 sts—46 sts. Work even for 3 rows, end on WS. **Inc Row 2:** Sc in first 2 sts, [work 2 sc in next st, sc in next 4 sts] 4 times, end work 2 sc in next st, sc in last 2 sts—50 sts. Work even until piece meaures 4½" from beg, end on WS. Fasten off. Turn work ready for a RS row.

Bodice
From RS, sk first 13 sts, join MC with a sc in next st, sc across next 23 sts—24 sts. Ch 1, turn. Dec 1 st each side on next row, then every row 4 times more—14 sts. Join CC, ch 1, turn. Work even for 2 rows. Ch 1, turn.

Left Strap
Work across first 2 sts. Ch 1, turn. Work even until strap measures 1¾" from beg. Fasten off.

Right Strap
From RS, sk next 10 sts, join CC with a sc in next st, sc in last st—2 sts. Ch 1, turn. Cont to work same as for left strap.

FINISHING
Beg at bottom edge, sew back seam to within 1⅝" of top edge. Sew straps to top back edges, ½" from back opening. Sew on snaps evenly spaced along back opening.

hat

STITCH GLOSSARY
CL = cluster st. To make a cluster st: yo, insert hook into st, [yo, draw up a lp, yo and draw through 2 lps on hook] 3 times, yo and draw through all 4 lps on hook.

With MC, ch 3. Join ch with a sl st forming a ring. **Rnd 1:** Work 6 sc over ch. Mark last st made with the safety pin. Unless stated otherwise, you will be working in a spiral marking the last st made with the safety pin to indicate end of rnd. **Rnd 2:** Work 2 sc in each st around—12 sts. **Rnd 3:** * Sc in next st, work 2 sc in next st, rep from * around—18 sts. **Rnd 4:** * Sc in next 2 sts, work 2 sc in next st, rep from * around—24 sts. **Rnd 5:** * Sc in next 3 sts, work 2 sc in next st, rep from * around—30 sts. **Rnd 6:** * Sc in next 4 sts, work 2 sc in next st, rep from * around—36 sts. **Rnd 7:** Working through back lps

materials

SHEATH

Yarn
Pearl Cotton #5 (25m/27.3yd) by DMC, 4 skeins #502 Blue Green (MC) and 2 skeins #310 Black (CC).

Crochet Hook
Size B (1) or size to obtain gauge.

Notions
Tapestry needle.
Small safety pin.
2 small metal snaps.

notes

1. When changing colors, draw new color through 2 lps on hook to complete sc.
2. Use a separate strand of CC for each vertical stripe.
3. Carry MC loosely across WS of work.

gauge

9 sc and 11 rows = 1".
FOR PROPER FIT, TAKE THE TIME TO CHECK YOUR GAUGE.

Afternoon Tea

Make both dress ensembles using size 5 pearl cotton. Fasten back openings with tiny metal snaps. Accent the wide-brimmed hat with a ribbon hat band and an elegant sheer ribbon rose.

only, sc in each st around. Work now through both lps. **Rnds 8 and 9:** Sc in each st around. **Rnd 10 (WS):** Ch 1, turn. * Sc in next 2 sts, CL in next st, rep from * around. Join rnd with a sl st in ch-1. **Rnds 11–13 (RS):** Rep rnd 8.

Brim

Rnd 14: * Sc in next st, work 2 sc in next st, rep from * around—54 sts. **Rnd 15:** Rep rnd 8. **Rnd 16:** * Sc in next 2 sts, work 2 sc in next st, rep from * around—72 sts. **Rnd 17:** Rep rnd 8. **Rnd 18 (RS):** * Sc in next 2 sts, CL in next st, rep from * around. Edge of brim will curl back showing CL sts on WS. Join rnd with a sl st in next st. Fasten off.

stylized stripes dress

Made in one piece beg with skirt. Skirt is made vertically. Beg at side edge, with A, ch 27. **Row 1:** Sc in 2nd ch from hook and in next ch, hdc in next 5 ch, dc in last 19 ch—26 sts. Ch 3, turn. **Row 2:** Dc in first 19 sts, hdc in next 5 sts, sc in last 2 sts. Join B, ch 1, turn. **Row 3:** Sc in first 2 sts, hdc in next 5 sts, dc in last 19 sts. Ch 3, turn. **Row 4:** Dc in first 19 sts, hdc in next 5 sts, sc in last 2 sts. Join A, ch 1, turn. **Row 5:** Rep row 3. **Row 6:** Rep row 4. Join B, ch 1, turn. Rep rows 3-6 until 8 B stripes have been completed. Ch 1, turn to sc edge.

Bodice

Foundation Row (RS): Work 31 sc evenly spaced across entire edge. Ch 1, turn. **Following Row:** Sc in each st across. Ch 1, turn. **Inc Row 1:** Sc in first 2 sts, [work 2 sc in next st, sc in next 4 sts] 5 times, work 2 sc in next st, sc in last 3 sts—37 sts. Ch 1, turn. **Following Row:** Sc in each st across. Ch 1, turn. **Inc Row 2:** Sc

in first 3 sts, [work 2 sc in next st, sc in next 4 sts] 6 times, work 2 sc in next st, sc in last 3 sts—44 sts. Ch 1, turn. **Next 3 Rows:** Sc in each st across. Ch 1, turn. **Inc Row 3:** Sc in first 3 sts, [work 2 sc in next st, sc in next 4 sts] 8 times—52 sts. Ch 1, turn. **Next 3 Rows:** Sc in each st across. Ch 1, turn. **Inc Row 4:** Sc in first 4 sts, [work 2 sc in next st, sc in next 5 sts] 8 times—60 sts. Ch 1, turn. **Next 5 Rows:** Sc in each st across. Ch 1, turn.

LEFT BACK

Sc across first 12 sts, ch 1, turn. Dec 1 st at armhole edge on next row, then every row once more—10 sts. Work even for 5 more rows. Fasten off.

FRONT

From RS, sk next 6 sts. Join B with a sc in next st, sc across next 23 sts—24 sts. Dec 1 st each side on next row, then every row twice more—18 sts. Work even for 4 more rows. Fasten off.

RIGHT BACK

From RS, sk next 6 sts. Join B with a sc in next st, sc across last 11 sts—12 sts. Dec 1 st at armhole edge on next row, then every row once more—10 sts. Work even for 5 more rows. Fasten off.

Collar

Foundation Row: From RS, join A with a sc in first st of left back, sc across next 9 sts, ch 5, sc across 18 sts of front, ch 5, sc across 10 sts of right back. Ch 3, turn. **Next Row:** Dc in each st and ch across—48 sts. Ch 3, turn. **Inc Row:** Dc in first 3 sts, [work 2 dc in next st, dc in next 4 sts] 9 times—57 sts. Ch 3, turn. **Next Row:** Dc in each st across. Ch 1, turn. **Last Row:** Sc in each st across. Fasten off.

106

FINISHING

Sew back skirt seam to within 1" of waist. Sew on snaps evenly spaced along back opening.

hat

With B, ch 3. Join ch with a sl st forming a ring. **Rnd 1:** Work 6 sc over ch. Mark last st made with the safety pin. You will be working in a spiral marking the last st made with the safety pin to indicate end of rnd. **Rnd 2:** Work 2 sc in each st around—12 sts. **Rnd 3:** * Sc in next st, work 2 sc in next st, rep from * around—18 sts. **Rnd 4:** * Sc in next 2 sts, work 2 sc in next st, rep from * around—24 sts. **Rnd 5:** * Sc in next 3 sts, work 2 sc in next st, rep from * around—30 sts. **Rnd 6:** * Sc in next 4 sts, work 2 sc in next st, rep from * around—36 sts. **Rnd 7:** Working through back lps only, sc in each st around. Work now through both lps. **Rnds 8–13:** Sc in each st around.
Brim
Rnd 14: * Sc in next st, work 2 sc in next st, rep from * around—54 sts. **Rnd 15:** Rep rnd 8. **Rnd 16:** * Sc in next 2 sts, work 2 sc in next st, rep from * around—72 sts. **Rnds 17 and 18:** Rep rnd 8. **Rnd 19:** * Sc in next 3 sts, work 2 sc in next st, rep from * around—90 sts. **Rnds 20 and 21:** Rep rnd 8. After rnd 21 is completed, join rnd with a sl st in next st. Fasten off.

FINISHING

Wrap ribbon around base of crown and criss cross ends; tack where ends cross to secure. Stitch rose where ends cross.

materials

STRIPED DRESS
Yarn
Pearl Cotton #5 (25m/27.3yd) by DMC, 2 skeins #642 Dk. Beige Gray (A) and 3 skeins #310 Black (B).
Crochet Hook
Size B (1) or size to obtain gauge.
Notions
Tapestry needle.
Small safety pin.
3 small metal snaps.
6"-length of ⅛"-wide black satin ribbon by Offray.
1 small Sheer Ribbon Rose #815 Cream by Offray.

notes

1. When changing colors, draw new color through 2 lps on hook to complete sc.
2. Carry color not in use loosely along side edge of work.

gauge

9 sc and 11 rows = 1".
FOR PROPER FIT, TAKE THE TIME TO CHECK YOUR GAUGE.

Sleek Sophistication

Every girl deserves a stately coat dress and Barbie® is no exception. This classic fashion is styled with all the right details: double-breasted button closure, notched collar and mock flap pockets.

coat dress

BODY

Made in one piece. Beg at bottom edge, with MC, ch 47. **Row 1 (WS):** Sc in 2nd ch from hook and in each ch across—46 sts. Ch 1, turn. **Row 2:** Sc in each st across. Ch 1, turn. Rep row 2 for pat st and work even until piece measures 2¾" from beg, end on WS. Ch 1, turn.

Shape Waist

Dec Row 1: Sc across first 11 sts, [dec 1 st over next 2 sts] twice, sc across next 16 sts, [dec 1 st over next 2 sts] twice, sc across last 11 sts—42 sts. Ch 1, turn. **Following Row:** Sc in each st across. Ch 1, turn. **Dec Row 2:** Sc across first 10 sts, [dec 1 st over next 2 sts] twice, sc across next 14 sts, [dec 1 st over next 2 sts] twice, sc across last 10 sts—38 sts. Ch 1, turn. **Following Row:** Sc in each st across. Ch 1, turn. **Dec Row 3:** Sc across first 9 sts, [dec 1 st over next 2 sts] twice, sc across next 12 sts, [dec 1 st over next 2 sts] twice, sc across last 9 sts—34 sts. Ch 1, turn. **Following Row:** Sc in each st across. Ch 1, turn. **Inc Row 1:** Sc across first 8 sts, [inc 1 st in next st] twice, sc across next 14 sts, [inc 1 st in next st] twice, sc across last 8 sts—38 sts. Ch 1, turn. **Following Row:** Sc in each st across. Ch 1, turn. **Inc Row**

2: Sc across first 9 sts, [inc 1 st in next st] twice, sc across next 16 sts, [inc 1 st in next st] twice, sc across last 9 sts—42 sts. Ch 1, turn. **Following Row:** Sc in each st across. Ch 1, turn. **Inc Row 3:** Sc across first 10 sts, [inc 1 st in next st] twice, sc across next 18 sts, [inc 1 st in next st] twice, sc across last 10 sts—46 sts. Ch 1, turn. **Following Row:** Sc in each st across. Ch 1, turn. **Inc Row 4:** Sc across first 12 sts, inc 1 st in next st, sc across next 20 sts, inc 1 st in next st, sc across last 12 sts—48 sts. Ch 1, turn. **Following Row:** Sc in each st across. Ch 1, turn. **Inc Row 5:** Sc across first 13 sts, inc 1 st in next st, sc across next 20 sts, inc 1 st in next st, sc across last 13 sts—50 sts. Ch 1, turn. **Following Row:** Sc in each st across. Ch 1, turn. Work even until piece measures 4¾" from beg, end on WS. Ch 1, turn.

Right Front

Work across first 12 sts. Ch 1, turn. Work even until piece measures 5¾" from beg, end on RS. Ch 1, turn.

Shape Neck

Work across first 6 sts. Ch 1, turn. Dec 1 st at neck edge on next row, then every row once more—4 sts. Ch 1, turn. Work even for 1 more row. Fasten off.

Yarn
True 4ply Botany (50g/170m) by Rowan, 1 ball each #582 Caramel (MC) and #546 Jet (CC).

Crochet Hook
Size C (2) or size to obtain gauge.

Notions
Tapestry needle.
4 black 6/0 "E" beads.

gauge

15 sc and 18 rows = 2".
FOR PROPER FIT, TAKE THE TIME TO CHECK YOUR GAUGE.

Sleek Sophistication

Make the dress in single crochet using a sport-weight wool in always popular tan and black.

BACK

From RS, sk next 5 underarm sts. Join MC with a sc in next st, sc across next 19 sts—20 sts. Work even until back measures same length as right front. Fasten off.

Left Front

From RS, sk next 5 underarm sts. Join MC with a sc in next st, sc across last 11 sts—12 sts. Ch 1, turn. Work even until piece measures 5¾" from beg, end on RS. Fasten off. Turn to WS.

Shape Neck

Sk first 8 sts, join MC with a sc in next st, sc across last 5 sts—6 sts. Ch 1, turn. Dec 1 st at neck edge on next row, then every row once more—4 sts. Ch 1, turn. Work even for 1 more row. Fasten off.

SLEEVES

Steam-press piece. Sew shoulder seams. From RS, work 20 sc evenly spaced around armhole edge. Ch 1, turn. Work even for 1", end on WS. Dec 1 st each side on next row, then every 6th row twice more—14 sts. Work even until sleeve measures 3⅛" from beg, end on WS. Fasten off.

FINISHING

Sew sleeve seams.

Collar

From RS join MC with a sc at first row of right neck shaping, work 19 more sc evenly spaced across neck edge to first row of left neck shaping—20 sts. Ch 1, turn. Work even for 4 more rows. Fasten off.

Front Edging

Row 1: From RS, join MC with a sc in side edge of first row of right front. Making sure that work lies flat, sc evenly along entire edge to first row of left front, working 2 sc in each corner. Fasten off. On each front, measure and mark 4¼" from bottom edge. Row 2: From WS, join CC with a sc in marked st on left front. Sc in each st to next marker, working 2 sc in each outer corner and sk across 2 sts in each inner corner to make sure edging lies flat. Fasten off. Steam-press edging.

Mock Pocket Flaps

(make 2)

With CC, ch 6. **Row 1:** Sc in 2nd ch from hook and in each ch across. Fasten off. Sew each flap on an angle as follows: Position (and pin) flap so that top edge is 3$\frac{1}{4}$" from bottom edge of dress and top side edge of flap is 1$\frac{1}{8}$" from front edge of dress. Now, position bottom side edge of flap so that it is 1$\frac{1}{4}$" from front edge. Using a running st, sew flap in place making sure it lies flat.

Sew on Bead Buttons

On left front, sew first bead 4$\frac{1}{8}$" from bottom edge of dress and $\frac{7}{8}$" from front edge of dress (this includes CC edging). Sew 2nd bead 4$\frac{1}{8}$" from bottom edge and $\frac{3}{8}$" from front edge. Sew 3rd bead 3$\frac{1}{4}$" from bottom edge of dress and $\frac{3}{4}$" from front edge of dress. Sew 4th bead 3$\frac{1}{4}$" from bottom edge and $\frac{1}{4}$" from front edge. To close dress, push beads between sts.

Haute Couture

This Seventh Avenue treasure can be paired with a dressy skirt for an evening out or with jeans for a casual Sunday in the park. It's made in a dainty eyelet stitch, with bold cluster stitches dotting the hem, cuffs and cowl collar. Make it in buttery yellow silk and cashmere yarn.

pullover

STITCH GLOSSARY

CL = cluster st. To make a cluster st: yo, insert hook into st, [yo, draw up a lp, yo and draw through 2 lps on hook] 3 times, yo and draw through all 4 lps on hook.

BACK

Beg at bottom edge, ch 28. **Row 1 (WS):** Sc in 2nd ch from hook and in each ch across—27 sts. Ch 1, turn. **Row 2:** Sc in each st across. Ch 1, turn. **Row 3:** Sc in first 3 sts, * CL in next st, sc in next 3 sts, rep from * across. Ch 1, turn. **Row 4:** Rep row 2. **Row 5:** Sc in first st, * CL in next st, sc in next 3 sts, rep from * across, end CL in next st, sc in last st. Ch 1, turn. **Row 6:** Rep row 2. **Row 7:** Rep row 3. **Row 8:** Rep row 2. **Row 9 (WS):** Sc in first st, * ch 1, sk next st, sc in next st, rep from * across. Ch 1, turn. **Row 10 (RS):** Sc in first st, * sc over next ch-1 sp, sc in next sc, rep from * across. Ch 1, turn. Rep rows 9 and 10 until piece measures 2¾" from beg, end on WS. Do not ch, turn.

Armholes

Sl st in first st, then over ch-1 sp and next sc, ch 1, work across to within last 3 sts (2 sc and 1 ch-1 sp)—21 sts. Ch 1, turn. Establish pat st as follows—**Row 11:** Sc in first 2 sts, * ch 1, sk next st, sc in next st, rep from * across, end sc in last st. Ch 1, turn. **Row 12:** Sc in first 2 sts, * sc over next ch-1 sp, sc in next sc, rep from * across, end sc in last st. Ch 1, turn. Rep rows 11 and 12 until piece measures 3¾" from beg, end on RS. Fasten off.

FRONT

Work same as for back.

LEFT SLEEVE

From RS, work 8 sc evenly spaced along left front armhole edge, ch 7, work 8 sc evenly spaced along left back armhole edge. Ch 1, turn. **Next Row (WS):** Sc in each st and ch across—23 sts. Ch 1, turn. **Following Row (RS):** Sc in each st across. Ch 1, turn. Rep rows 9 and 10 same as for back until sleeve measures ¾" from beg, end on WS. Keeping to pat st, dec 1 st each side on next row, then every 4th row 3 times more—15 sts. Work even until sleeve measures 2½" from beg, end on RS. Rep rows 3-8 same as for back. Fasten off.

RIGHT SLEEVE

From RS, work 8 sc evenly spaced along right back armhole edge, ch 7, work 8 sc evenly spaced along right front armhole edge. Ch 1, turn. Cont to work same as for left sleeve.

FINISHING

Sew side and sleeve seams.

Collar

From RS, sk first 10 sts of top back edge, join yarn with a sc in next st, sc in next 10 sts, work 1 sc in each of 7 bottom ch lps of first sleeve, sc in next 21 sts of top front edge, work 1 sc in each of 7 bottom ch lps of next sleeve, sc in next 9 sts of back, work 2 sc in last st—57 sts. Ch 1, turn. **Next Row:** Sc in each st across. Ch 1, turn. Rep rows 9 and 10 same as for back until collar measures ⅞" from beg, end on row 9. **Inc Row:** Keeping to pat st, inc 10 sts evenly spaced across—67 sts. Rep rows 3-8 same as for back. Fasten off. Sew collar seam.

materials

Yarn
Richesse et Soie (25g/approx 145yd) by K1C2, 1 ball #9401 Butter.
Crochet Hook
Size C (2) or size to obtain gauge.
Notions
Tapestry needle.

gauge

6 sts = 1" (in pat st).
FOR PROPER FIT, TAKE THE TIME TO CHECK YOUR GAUGE.

Granny Square Update

These colorful crocheted squares were first worn as clothing in the 70's and have now come full circle. Tiny motifs are made using a fine wool yarn in a garden of colors. Surrounding the flower center with green gives the illusion of leaves and edging them with black makes the colors pop. This eye-dazzling set includes a cute cropped top and a darling dirndl skirt. Leave bottom squares of the skirt unstitched to give the hem an extra little kick.

cropped top

Make 10 granny squares in the following flower colors: 2 B, 3 C, 1 D, 2 E, 1 F and 1 G.

GRANNY SQUARE

With flower color, ch 6. Join ch with a sl st forming a ring. **Rnd 1 (RS):** Ch 3 (always counts as 1 dc), work 2 dc over ring, ch 2, * work 3 dc over ring, ch 2, rep from * 3 times. Join rnd with a sl st in 3rd ch of ch-3. Fasten off. Turn square so WS is facing you. Join A with a sl st in any ch-2 sp. **Rnd 2 (WS):** Ch 3, work 2 dc in same ch-2 sp, ch 1, * work (3 dc, ch 2, 3 dc) in next ch-2 sp, ch 1, rep from * 3 times, end with 3 dc in beg ch-2 sp, ch 2. Join rnd with a sl st in 3rd ch of ch-3. Fasten off. Turn square so RS is facing you. Join MC with a sl st in any ch-2 sp. **Rnd 3 (RS):** Ch 3, work 2 dc in same ch-2 sp, ch 1, * work 3 dc in next ch-1 sp, ch 1, work (3 dc, ch 2, 3 dc) in next ch-2 sp, ch 1, rep from * 3 times, end with 3 dc in next ch-1 sp, ch 1, 3 dc in beg ch-2 sp, ch 2. Join rnd with a sl st in 3rd ch of ch-3. Fasten off leaving a 10"-long tail for sewing.

FINISHING
Referring to Assembly Diagram for Cropped Top, sew squares together. Sew side seams.

skirt

Make 30 granny squares in the following flower colors: 4 B, 4 C, 5 D, 6 E, 6 F and 5 G.

FINISHING
Referring to Assembly Diagram for Skirt, sew vertical columns of squares together first. Sew columns together, leaving side edges of first row of squares unstitched.

Waist Edging
From RS, join MC with a sl st in first ch-2 sp at top right edge, ch 3. **Row 1:** Sk every ch sp, dc in each dc across. Ch 3, turn. **Row 2:** Dc in first 3 sts, * sk next dc, dc in next 3 sts, rep from * across. Fasten off.
Beg 1 square from bottom edge, sew back seam to within 1 square of top edge. Run elastic thread through last row of waist edging; fasten off securely. Sew snap to waist opening.

materials

Yarn
Broder Medicis Tapestry Wool (27.3yd/25m) by DMC, 4 skeins Black (MC), 2 skeins #8419 Avocado (A) and 1 skein of each flower color: #8209 Very Lt. Colonial Blue (B), #8153 Fuchsia (C), #8397 Lt. Lavender (D), #8026 Yellow (E), #8134 Peach (F) and #8896 Med. Lavender.

Crochet Hook
Steel crochet hook size 8 or size to obtain gauge.

Notions
Tapestry needle.
1 small metal snap.
Black elastic thread.

C	E	D
B		C
C		G
B	E	F

ASSEMBLY DIAGRAM FOR CROPPED TOP AND SKIRT

C	G	D	F	E	F
E	F	E	B	G	D
G	B	G	D	F	E
F	E	F	C	B	G
B	C	D	E	D	C

gauge

Each granny square measures 1" x 1".
FOR PROPER FIT, TAKE THE TIME TO CHECK YOUR GAUGE.

Glamorous Crisscross Silhouette

Barbie® steals the show in this enchanting evening number. The long, sleek gown is made in a shimmering metallic yarn. It features dramatic crisscross straps that fasten at the back neck with a sparkling bead button. Ever-so-chic, this double crochet stole makes an extravagant accompaniment.

gown

Made in one piece. Beg at bottom edge with A, ch 43. **Row 1 (WS):** Sc in 2nd ch from hook and in each ch across—42 sts. Ch 1, turn. **Row 2:** Sc in each st across. Ch 1, turn. Rep row 2 for pat st and work even until piece measures 5¾" from beg, end on WS. Ch 1, turn.

Shape Waist

Dec Row (RS): Sc in first 2 sts, [dec 1 st over next 2 sts, sc in next 3 sts] 8 times—34 sts. Work even for 4 rows, end on RS. **Inc Row (WS):** Sc in first 2 sts, [inc 1 st in next st, sc in next 3 sts] 8 times—42 sts. Work even for 2 rows.

Divide for Front Opening
Left Front—Next Row (RS): Work across first 21 sts. Ch 1, turn. Work even for 7 more rows, end on WS. Fasten off. Turn work ready for a RS row. **Next Row (RS):** Sk first 12 sts, join yarn with a sc in next st, finish row—9 sts. Ch 1, turn. **Dec Row:** Work across to within last 2 sts, dec 1 st over last 2 sts (arm edge). Ch 1, turn. Continue to dec 1 st at same edge every row 5 times more—3 sts (strap). Work even for 11 more rows. Fasten off.

Right Front
Next Row (RS): Join yarn with a sc in next st, finish row—21 sts. Ch 1, turn. Work even for 7 more rows, end on WS. Ch 1, turn. **Next Row (RS):** Work across first 9 sts. Ch 1, turn. **Dec Row:** Dec 1 st at beg of next row (arm edge). Ch 1, turn. Continue to dec 1 st at same edge every row 5 times more—3 sts (strap). Work even for 11 more rows. Fasten off.

FINISHING
Beg 2" from bottom edge, sew back seam to within ½" of waist shaping. Sew 4 bead buttons evenly spaced along left back opening. To close back, push beads between sts of right back opening. Sew 1 bead to end of right strap. To secure straps, push bead between sts on last row of left strap.

stole

With B, ch 14. **Row 1:** Dc in 4th ch from hook and in each ch across—11 sts. Ch 3, turn. **Row 2:** Dc in each st across. Ch 3, turn. Rep row 2 for pat st and work even until piece measures 12½" from beg. Fasten off. Draw in all loose ends.

materials

Yarn
A Taste of Glitz (25g/190yd) by K1C2, 1 cone #4 Creme de Menthe (A) and Artic Rays (8yd/7.3m) by Rainbow Gallery, 4 cards #AR8 Tree Green (B).
Crochet Hook
Size C (2) or size to obtain gauges.
Notions
Tapestry needle.
5 dark green transparent 6/0 "E" beads.

gauges

8 sc = 1" (using A).
7 dc = 1" (using B).
FOR PROPER FIT, TAKE THE TIME TO CHECK YOUR GAUGE.

backpack

BOTTOM

Made in one piece. Beg at base of backpack, ch 15. **Row 1 (WS):** Sc in 2nd ch from hook and in each ch across—14 sts. Ch 1, turn. **Rows 2-6:** Sc in each st across. Ch 1, turn. After row 6 is completed, fasten off. Turn ready for a RS row. **Rnd 1:** Sk first 7 sts of top edge, join yarn with a sc in next st, sc in next 6 sts. Turn to side edge, work 6 sc evenly spaced across. Turn to bottom lps of ch, work 1 sc in each of 14 bottom lps across. Turn to side edge, work 6 sc evenly spaced across. Turn to top edge, sc in 7 sts— 40 sts. Mark last st made with the safety pin to indicate end of rnd (this is the back of the backpack). Join rnd with a sl st in first sc. **Rnd 2:** Ch 1, sc in each st around. Join rnd with a sl st in ch-1. Rep rnd 2 until 1⅝" from beg. Fasten off.

FLAP

Beg at bottom edge, ch 11. **Row 1 (WS):** Sc in 2nd ch from hook and in each ch across—10 sts. Ch 1, turn. **Rows 2-8:** Sc in each st across. Ch 1, turn. **Row 9 (buttonhole row):** Sc in first 4 sts, ch 2, sk next 2 sts, sc in last 4 sts. Ch 1, turn. **Row 10:** Sc in first 4 sts, work 2 sc over ch-2, sc in last 4 sts. Fasten off.

FINISHING

Sew bottom edge of flap to center top back edge of backpack. Sew on bead to correspond to buttonhole.
Straps
Leaving a long end, tightly crochet a ch to measure 9"-long. Fasten off leaving a long end. Thread one end into tapestry needle. Button flap. With front of backpack facing you, push in top right side edge ¼" to pleat it; pin to secure. Unbutton flap. Working from front to back, insert needle ⅛" from top edge and ⅛" from side edge of backpack; draw strap through all thicknesses. Turn backpack so back is facing you. Insert needle through rnd 1, ⅛" from left side edge. On inside of backpack, knot end of ch; trim off excess yarn. Thread opposite end of strap into tapestry needle. Repeat on left side edge of backpack.

string bag

BACK

Working tightly and evenly, work 40 sc over bone ring. Join rnd with a sl st in first st. Ch 1, turn. **Foundation Row (WS):** Sc in next 14 sts. Ch 2, turn. **Row 1:** Hdc in first st, [ch 3, sk next st, sc in next st] 6 times, end hdc in last st—6 ch-3 lps. Ch 2, turn. **Row 2:** Hdc in first st, [ch 3, sc in next ch-3 lp] 6 times, end hdc in last st. Ch 2, turn. Rep row 2 for pat st and work 8 times more. Ch 1, turn. **Next Row:** Sc in first 2 sts, * work 2 sc over next ch-3 lp, sc in next st,

---

With a sporty new backpack slung over her shoulders, Barbie® is set for the entire year.

Made with size 5 pearl cotton yarn and single crochet.

Make a roomy string bag for grocery shopping. Crocheted in a mesh stitch using two bone rings for the handles.

The tote is made in one continuous piece in an easy double crochet V-stitch.

rep from * across—20 sts. Ch 1, turn. **Following Row:** Sc in each st across. Ch 1, turn. Rep last row once more. Fasten off.

FRONT

Work same as for back.

FINISHING

Sew bottom seam. Beg at bottom edge, sew side seams for 1".

mesh tote

Made in one piece. Beg at bottom of tote, ch 20. **Foundation Row:** Sc in 2nd ch from hook and in each ch across—19 sts. Ch 1, turn. **Rnd 1:** Ch 3 (always counts as 1 dc), dc in next st, [sk next st, work (dc, ch 1, dc) in next st] 8 times, sk next st, dc in last st. Turn to side edge of foundation row, work 1 dc in side edge. Turn to bottom of foundation row. Working through lps of beg ch, work 1 dc in first lp, [sk next lp, work (dc, ch 1, dc) in next lp] 8 times, end sk next lp, dc in last lp. Join rnd with a sl st in 3rd ch of ch-3. **Rnd 2:** Ch 3, dc in first dc, [work (dc, ch 1, dc) in next ch-1 sp] 8 times, dc in next 3 dc, rep between [ ]'s 8 times, end dc in last dc. Join rnd with a sl st in 3rd ch of ch-3. Rep this rnd 6 times more.

Handles

Rnd 1: Ch 1, sc in next dc, [work 3 sc over next ch-1 sp] 8 times, sc in each of next 3 dc, rep between [ ]'s 8 times, end sc in last dc—52 sts. Join rnd with a sl st in ch-1. **Rnd 2:** Ch 1, sc in first 8 sts, ch 12, sk next 10 sts, sc in next 16 sts, ch 12, sk next 10 sts, end sc in last 8 sts. Join rnd with a sl st in ch-1. **Rnd 3:** Ch 1, sc in first 8 sts, work 12 sc over ch-12, sc in next 16 sts, work 12 sc over ch-10, end sc in last 8 sts. Join rnd with a sl st in ch-1. **Rnd 4:** Ch 1, sc in each st around. Join rnd with a sl st in ch-1. Fasten off.

FINISHING

Draw in all loose ends.

materials

BACKPACK

Yarn

Size 5 Perle Cotton (25m/27.3yd) by DMC, 1 skein #322 Dk. Dk. Baby Blue.

Crochet Hook

Size B (1) or size to obtain gauge.

Notions

Tapestry needle.
1 small safety pin.
1 gold metallic 6/0 "E" bead.

STRING BAG

Yarn

Cebelia Size 10 Crochet Cotton (260m/284yd) by DMC, 1 ball #743 Med. Yellow.

Crochet Hook

Size 4 steel crochet hook or size to obtain gauge.

Notions

Tapestry needle.
2 (¾"/19mm) Luxite "Bone Rings" by Susan Bates.

MESH TOTE

Yarn

Cebelia Size 10 Crochet Cotton (260m/284yd) by DMC, 1 ball #816 Garnet.

Crochet Hook

Size 4 steel crochet hook or size to obtain gauge.

Notions

Tapestry needle.

gauges

BACKPACK

10 sc and 10 rnds = 1"

STRING BAG

10 sc = 1".

MESH TOTE

10 sc = 1".
TAKE THE TIME TO CHECK YOUR GAUGE.

Fashionable Hat Sets

This alluring "fur" hat set embraces sheer luxury. Worked in single crochet, make the crown in elegant cashmere and the brim in exquisite angora. Complete the look with a matching scarf. Made of real jute, an all-natural fiber, this whimsical combo features impeccable details, right down to the tiny tassels. The weight of the cord makes these easy-crochet accessories a quick project.

"fur" hat

With smaller hook and A, ch 3. Join ch with a sl st forming a ring. **Rnd 1:** Work 6 sc over ch. Mark last st made with the safety pin. You will be working in a spiral marking the last st made with the safety pin to indicate end of rnd. **Rnd 2:** Work 2 sc in each st around—12 sts. **Rnd 3:** * Sc in next st, work 2 sc in next st, rep from * around—18 sts. **Rnd 4:** * Sc in next 2 sts, work 2 sc in next st, rep from * around—24 sts. **Rnd 5:** * Sc in next 3 sts, work 2 sc in next st, rep from * around—30 sts. **Rnd 6:** * Sc in next 4 sts, work 2 sc in next st, rep from * around—36 sts. **Rnds 7–13:** Sc in each st around. After rnd 13 is completed, remove safety pin marker. Join B, change to larger hook, ch 1.

Fur Brim

Rnds 14 and 15: Sc in each st around. Join rnd with a sl st in ch-1. Ch 1, turn. **Rnd 16:** * Sc in next 2 sts, work 2 sc in next st, rep from * around—48 sts. Join rnd with a sl st in ch-1. Ch 1, turn. **Rnd 17:** Sc in each st around. Join rnd with a sl st in ch-1. Fasten off.

"fur" scarf

Scarf is made vertically. Beg at long side edge, with larger hook and B, ch 55. **Row 1:** Sc in 2nd ch from hook and in each ch across—54 sts. Ch 1, turn. **Rows 2–4:** Sc in each st across. Ch 1, turn. After row 4 is completed, fasten off.

jute hat

Make a lp 8" from free end of jute. Sl lp onto hook. **Foundation Row:** Work 6 sc over free end of jute. Mark last st made with the safety pin. You will be working in a spiral marking the last st made with the safety pin to indicate end of rnd. **Rnd 1:** With top lps of sts facing you, curl row of sts towards the left so that first sc made is at your left. Working through back lps, work 2 sc in first st and in each of next 5 sts—12 sts. To close opening at top of hat, pull free end of jute. Continue to work through back lps only. **Rnd 2:** * Sc in next st, work 2 sc in next st, rep from * around—18 sts. **Rnd 3:**

* Sc in next 2 sts, work 2 sc in next st, rep from * around—24 sts. **Rnds 4 to 7:** Sc in each st around.

Brim

Rnd 8: Work 2 sc in each st around—48 sts. **Rnds 9-11:** Sc in each st around. After rnd 11 is completed, sl st in next st. Fasten off.

FINISHING

Draw in loose ends. Trim away any long, loose fibers.

Hatband

Cut 3 (20"-long) strands of jute. With ends even, make an overhand knot at one end, then knot again 2" from first knot. Working tightly, braid for 7¼"; make a knot at base of braid. Trim off excess jute at each end, ½" from knots. Tie hatband around hat, as shown.

jute bag

Ch 16. **Foundation Rnd:** Sc in back lp of 2nd ch from hook, then sc in back lp of next 14 ch. Turn work so that unworked lps of ch are now at top. Sc in each of 15 ch—30 sts. Mark last st made with the safety pin. You will be working in a spiral marking the last st made with the safety pin to indicate end of rnd. **Rnd 1:** Working through back lps only, sc in each st around. Rep this rnd until bag measures 1¾" from beg. **Last Rnd:** Working through both lps, sc in each st around. Join rnd with a sl st. Fasten off.

FINISHING

Draw in loose ends. Trim away any long, loose fibers.

Handles

(make 2)

Cut 6 (20"-long) strands of jute. With ends even, make an overhand knot at one end, then knot again 2" from first knot. Working tightly, braid pairs of strands for 4½"; make a knot at base of braid. Trim off excess jute at each end, ¾" from knots. Using a single strand of jute, sew handles (above knots) to each side of bag, as shown.

materials

"FUR" HAT AND SCARF

Yarn

Rainbow Cashmere (9yd/8.2m) by Rainbow Gallery, 2 cards #H18 Brown (A) and Rainbow Angora (7yd/6.4m) also by Rainbow Gallery, 3 cards #RA21 Brown (B).

Crochet Hooks

Size C (2) and D (3) or sizes to obtain gauges.

Notions

Tapestry needle. Small safety pin.

JUTE HAT AND BAG

Yarn

1 Ply #20 Jute Jewelry Cord (133yd) by ME Enterprises, 1 spool.

Crochet Hook

Size C (2) or size to obtain gauge.

Notions

Large tapestry needle. Small safety pin.

note

JUTE HAT AND BAG

Jute is dotted with imperfections. Simply remove them as you come across them.

gauges

"FUR" HAT AND SCARF

9 sc = 1" (using A and smaller hook).

5 sc = 1" (using B and larger hook).

JUTE HAT AND BAG

6 sc and 6 rows = 1".

FOR PROPER FIT, TAKE THE TIME TO CHECK YOUR GAUGE.

Cold Weather Accoutrements

Barbie® warms up to winter in a fabulous tweed set. The military-style hat is made in a rectangle that gets stitched together. The chill-chasing pull-through scarf works up quickly in single crochet. This beautiful blue hat and scarf will keep Barbie® cozy on the ice. Decorate the top of the hat and ends of the scarf with lots of tiny acrylic pompoms.

warm 'n tweedy hat

Beg at bottom edge, ch 29. **Row 1:** Sc in 2nd ch from hook and in each ch across—28 sts. Ch 1, turn. **Row 2:** Sc in each st across. Ch 1, turn. Rep row 2 for pat st and work even until piece measures 2" from beg. Fasten off.

FINISHING

Fold piece in half widthwise, then sew edges of last row together. Beg at bottom edge, sew side seam for ½" with WS facing, then sew remaining seam with RS facing. Turn bottom edge up ½".

pull through scarf

Scarf is made vertically. Beg at long side edge, ch 49. **Row 1:** Sc in 2nd ch from hook and in each ch across—48 sts. Ch 1, turn. **Row 2:** Sc in each st across. Ch 1, turn. Rep row 2 for pat st and work even for 2 more rows. **Next Row:** Sc in first 9 sts, ch 4, sk next 4 sts, sc in last 35 sts. Ch 1, turn. **Following Row:** Sc in first 35 sts, work 4 sc over ch-4, sc in last 9 sts. Ch 1, turn. Work even for 3 more rows. Fasten off.

FINISHING

Draw in all loose ends. Lightly steam-press scarf.

pompom hat

Made vertically. Beg at side edge, ch 18. **Row 1 (WS):** Sc in 2nd ch from hook and in next 2 ch, hdc in next 4 ch, dc in last 10 ch—17 sts. Ch 3, turn. **Row 2:** Dc in first 10 sts, hdc in next 4 sts, sc in last 3 sts. Ch 1, turn. **Row 3:** Sc in first 3 sts, hdc in next 4 sts, dc in last 10 sts. Ch 3, turn. Rep rows 2 and 3 until dc edge measures 4¾" from beg. Fasten off.

FINISHING

Beg at dc edge, sew side seam for ½" with WS facing, then sew remaining seam with RS facing. Sew a gathering thread around top, then pull to gather; fasten off securely. Sew 3 pompoms to center top of hat. Turn up bottom edge ½".

pompom scarf

Beg at bottom edge, ch 9. **Row 1:** Sc in 2nd ch from hook and in each ch across—8 sts. Ch 3, turn. **Row 2:** Dc in each st across. Ch 3, turn. Rep row 2 for pat st and work even until piece measures 12" from beg, ch 1, turn. **Last Row:** Sc in each st across. Fasten off.

FINISHING

Sew 5 pompoms evenly spaced across each end of scarf.

WARM 'N TWEEDY SET
Yarn
Rowanspun 4ply (25g/162yd) by Rowan, 1 hank #707 Blood.
Crochet Hook
Size C (2) or size to obtain gauge.
Notions
Tapestry needle.
POMPOM SET
Yarn
Paternayan 3 Ply Persian Wool (approx 8yd) by JCA, 2 skeins #545 Lt. Cobalt Blue.
Crochet Hook
Size C (2) or size to obtain gauge.
Notions
Tapestry needle.
Sewing needle.
Light blue sewing thread.
13 (5mm) light blue acrylic pompoms.

note

POMPOM SET
Use 1 ply of yarn throughout.

gauges

WARM 'N TWEEDY SET
7 sc = 1".
POMPOM SET
8 dc and 4 rows = 1" (using 1 ply of yarn).
FOR PROPER FIT, TAKE THE TIME TO CHECK YOUR GAUGE.

Hats For All Occasions

These chic chapeaux are quick and easy to make and require only one skein of size 5 pearl cotton for each. Make a charming ruby bowler. It's worked in a richly textured moss stitch and is accented with a black ribbon hat band. For a touch of the highlands, a Scottish tam that sports a little feather. This cute cloche is the perfect accessory for spring and summer fashions.

ruby bowler

Ch 3. Join ch with a sl st forming a ring. **Rnd 1:** Work 6 sc over ch. Mark last st made with the safety pin. You will be working in a spiral marking the last st made with the safety pin to indicate end of rnd. **Rnd 2:** Work 2 sc in each st around—12 sts. **Rnd 3:** * Sc in next st, work 2 sc in next st, rep from * around—18 sts. **Rnd 4:** * Sc in next 2 sts, work 2 sc in next st, rep from * around—24 sts. **Rnd 5:** * Sc in next 3 sts, work 2 sc in next st, rep from * around—30 sts. **Rnd 6:** * Sc in next 4 sts, work 2 sc in next st, rep from * around—36 sts. **Rnds 7, 9 and 11:** * Dc in next st, sc in next st, rep from * around. **Rnds 8, 10 and 12:** * Sc in next st, dc in next st, rep from * around.

BRIM
Rnd 13: * Sc in next st, work 2 sc in next st, rep from * around—54 sts. **Rnds 14 and 16:** * Dc in next st, sc in next st, rep from * around. **Rnds 15 and 17:** * Sc in next st, dc in next st, rep from * around. After rnd 17 is completed, join rnd with a sl st in next st. Fasten off.

FINISHING
Draw in all loose ends.
Wrap ribbon around base of crown, overlapping ends. Fold top end under, then sew through all layers of ribbon to secure in place.

tam-'o-shanter

Worked from the WS. Ch 3. Join ch with a sl st forming a ring. **Rnd 1:** Work 6 sc over ch. Mark last st made with the safety pin. You will be working in a spiral marking the last st made with the safety pin to indicate end of rnd. **Rnd 2:** Work 2

sc in each st around—12 sts. **Rnd 3:** * Sc in next st, work 2 sc in next st, rep from * around—18 sts. **Rnd 4:** * Sc in next 2 sts, work 2 sc in next st, rep from * around—24 sts. **Rnd 5:** * Sc in next 3 sts, work 2 sc in next st, rep from * around—30 sts. **Rnd 6:** * Sc in next 4 sts, work 2 sc in next st, rep from * around—36 sts. **Rnd 7:** * Sc in next 5 sts, work 2 sc in next st, rep from * around—42 sts. **Rnd 8:** * Sc in next 6 sts, work 2 sc in next st, rep from * around—48 sts. **Rnd 9:** * Sc in next 7 sts, work 2 sc in next st, rep from * around—54 sts. **Rnd 10:** * Sc in next 8 sts, work 2 sc in next st, rep from * around—60 sts. **Rnds 11-13:** Work even around. **Rnd 14:** * Sc in next 4 sts, dec 1 st over next 2 sts, rep from * around—50 sts. **Rnd 15:** * Sc in next 3 sts, dec 1 st over next 2 sts, rep from * around—

40 sts. **Rnd 16:** * Sc in next 2 sts, dec 1 st over next 2 sts, rep from * around—30 sts. **Rnd 17:** Work even around. Turn tam RS out. **Rnd 18:** Working from left to right, sc in each st around. Join rnd with a sl st in next st. Fasten off.

FINISHING
Draw in all loose ends. Referring to photo, sew on bead, then thread feather through hole in bead.

cute cloche

Ch 3. Join ch with a sl st forming a ring. **Rnd 1:** Work 6 sc over ch. Mark last st made with the safety pin. You will be working in a spiral marking the last st made with the safety pin to indicate end of rnd. Work through back lps only unless stated otherwise. **Rnd 2:** Work 2 sc in each st around—12 sts. **Rnd 3:** * Sc in next st, work 2 sc in next st, rep from * around—18 sts. **Rnd 4:** * Sc in next 2 sts, work 2 sc in next st, rep from * around—24 sts. **Rnd 5:** * Sc in next 3 sts, work 2 sc in next st, rep from * around—30 sts. **Rnd 6:** * Sc in next 4 sts, work 2 sc in next st, rep from * around—36 sts. **Rnds 7-12:** Sc in each st around.

BRIM
Rnd 13: Working through both lps, * sc in next st, work 2 sc in next st, rep from * around—54 sts. **Rnds 14 and 15:** Working through back lps only, sc in each st around. After rnd 15 is completed, join rnd with a sl st in next st. Fasten off.
FINISHING
Draw in all loose ends.

materials

RUBY BOWLER
Yarn
Pearl Cotton #5 (25m/27.3yd) by DMC, 1 skein #814 Dk. Garnet.
Crochet Hook for all hats
Size B (1) or size to obtain gauge.
Notions
Tapestry needle.
Sewing needle.
Small safety pin.
Black sewing thread.
5¼"-length of ⅛"-wide black satin ribbon by Offray.
TAM-'O-SHANTER
Yarn
Pearl Cotton #5 (25m/27.3yd) by DMC, 1 skein #832 Golden Olive.
Notions
Tapestry needle.
Sewing needle.
Small safety pin.
Dark gold sewing thread.
1 brown translucent 6/0 "E" bead.
1 (2"-long) pheasant feather.
CUTE CLOCHE
Yarn
Pearl Cotton #5 (25m/27.3yd) by DMC, 1 skein #367 Dk. Pistachio Green.
Notions
Tapestry needle.
Small safety pin.

gauge

ALL HATS
9 sc = 1".
FOR PROPER FIT, TAKE THE TIME TO CHECK YOUR GAUGE.

Hats For All Occasions

Sophisticated stripes make a picture perfect hat. Make it in single crochet using two contrasting colors. Add a sheer ribbon rose for a dash of drama. Complete the collection with a wide-brimmed hat that's bold with gold beads. Make it in single crochet, working in rounds of beads as you go.

picture hat

With A, ch 3. Join ch with a sl st forming a ring. **Rnd 1:** Work 6 sc over ch. Join B. Mark last st made with the safety pin. You will be working in a spiral marking the last st made with the safety pin to indicate end of rnd. Change to next color at end of each rnd. Work all of the following rnds working through back lp of each st. **Rnd 2:** With B, work 2 sc in each st around—12 sts. **Rnd 3:** With A, * sc in next st, work 2 sc in next st, rep from * around—

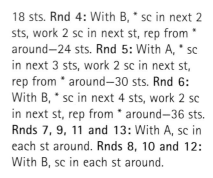

18 sts. **Rnd 4:** With B, * sc in next 2 sts, work 2 sc in next st, rep from * around—24 sts. **Rnd 5:** With A, * sc in next 3 sts, work 2 sc in next st, rep from * around—30 sts. **Rnd 6:** With B, * sc in next 4 sts, work 2 sc in next st, rep from * around—36 sts. **Rnds 7, 9, 11 and 13:** With A, sc in each st around. **Rnds 8, 10 and 12:** With B, sc in each st around.

BRIM

Rnd 14: With B, * sc in next st, work 2 sc in next st, rep from * around—54 sts. **Rnd 15:** With A, sc in each st around. **Rnd 16:** With B, * sc in next 2 sts, work 2 sc in next st, rep from * around—72 sts. **Rnd 17:** With A, sc in each st around. **Rnd 18:** With B, sc in each st around. Join rnd with a sl st in next st. Fasten off.

FINISHING

Draw in all loose ends. Referring to photo, sew ribbon rose in place.

beautifully beaded hat

STITCH GLOSSARY

Bst = bead st. Worked on WS rows. Insert hook into st. Slide a bead all the way up lead yarn to hook. Going under lead yarn, hook lead yarn that's coming out of left side of bead and draw up a lp. Yo and draw through both lps on hook.

Using big eye needle, string beads onto yarn. Ch 3. Join ch with a sl st forming a ring. **Rnd 1:** Work 6 sc over ch. Mark last st made with the safety pin. Except where noted, you will be working in a spiral marking the last st made with the safety pin to indicate end of rnd. **Rnd 2:** Work 2 sc in each st around—12 sts. **Rnd 3:** * Sc in next st, work 2 sc in next st, rep from * around—18 sts. **Rnd 4:** * Sc in next 2 sts, work 2 sc in next st, rep from * around—24 sts. **Rnd 5:** * Sc in next 3 sts, work 2 sc in next st, rep from * around—30 sts. **Rnd 6:**

* Sc in next 4 sts, work 2 sc in next st, rep from * around—36 sts. **Rnd 7:** Sc in each st around. Remove safety pin. Ch 1, turn to WS. **Rnd 8 (WS):** Bst in each st around. Join rnd with a sl st in ch-1. Mark last st made with safety pin. Turn to RS. **Rnds 9–13:** Sc in each st around. After rnd 13 is completed, remove safety pin. Ch 1, turn to WS. **Rnd 14 (WS):** Rep rnd 8. Mark last st made with safety pin. Turn to RS.

BRIM

Rnd 15: * Sc in next st, work 2 sc in next st, rep from * around—54 sts. **Rnd 16:** Sc in each st around. **Rnd 17:** * Sc in next 2 sts, work 2 sc in next st, rep from * around—72 sts. **Rnd 18:** Sc in each st around. Remove safety pin. Ch 1, turn to WS. **Rnd 19 (WS):** Rep rnd 8. Join rnd with a sl st in ch-1. Fasten off.

FINISHING

Draw in all loose ends. For each rnd of beads, work as follows: Thread big eye needle with a 20"-length of yarn. Have cut ends of yarn even, so you'll be working with a double strand. Beg at back of hat, run needle through beads. Fasten off ends on WS.

materials

PICTURE HAT

Yarn
Pearl Cotton #5 (25m/27.3yd) by DMC, 1 skein each #310 Black (A) and #613 Very Lt. Drab Brown (B).

Crochet Hook for all hats
Size B (1) or size to obtain gauge.

Notions
Tapestry needle.
Sewing needle.
Small safety pin.
Black sewing thread.
1 small Ribbon Rose #168 Colonial Rose by Offray.

BEADED HAT

Yarn
Pearl Cotton #5 (25m/27.3yd) by DMC, 1 skein #336 Navy Blue.

Notions
Tapestry needle.
2½"-long Big Eye Needle.
144 (3mm) gold pearls.
Small safety pin.

notes

PICTURE HAT

1. When changing color, draw new color though 2 lps on hook to complete last sc of rnd.
2. Carry color not in use loosely along WS of hat.

gauge

ALL HATS

9 sc = 1".
FOR PROPER FIT, TAKE THE TIME TO CHECK YOUR GAUGE.

Ballerina Dream Surplice

This sweet sweater is a reflection of Barbie® and her good taste. The piece is made in single crochet using a pretty almond pink crochet cotton. This waist-length top also features long sleeves and side ties. The perfect top to keep Barbie® warm between ballet classes.

surplice

BACK

Beg at bottom edge, ch 17. **Row 1 (RS):** Sc in 2nd ch from hook and in each ch across—16 sts. Ch 1, turn. **Row 2:** Sc in each st across. Ch 1, turn. Rep row 2 for pat st and work even for 2 more rows, end on WS.

Shape Sides

Inc 1 st each side on next row, then every other row 3 times more—24 sts. Work even until piece measures 1¾" from beg, end on WS. Do not ch, turn.

Armholes

Sl st across first 3 sts, ch 1, work across to within last 3 sts—18 sts. Ch 1, turn. Work even until piece measures 3" from beg. Fasten off.

LEFT FRONT

Beg at bottom edge, ch 15. **Row 1 (RS):** Sc in 2nd ch from hook and in each ch across—14 sts. Ch 1, turn. **Row 2:** Sc in each st across. Ch 1, turn. Rep row 2 for pat st.

Shape Neck and Side

Dec 1 st at end of next row, then at same edge every other row 11 times more, AT THE SAME TIME, when 2 rows have been completed, inc 1 st at side edge on next row, then every other row 3 times more. Work until piece measures 1¾" from beg, end on WS.

Armhole

Work across to within last 3 sts. Ch 1, turn. After all neck dec have been completed, work even on 3 sts until piece measures same length as back. Fasten off.

RIGHT FRONT

Beg at bottom edge, ch 15. **Row 1 (RS):** Sc in 2nd ch from hook and in each ch across—14 sts. Ch 1, turn.

Row 2: Sc in each st across. Ch 1, turn. Rep row 2 for pat st.

Shape Neck and Side

Dec 1 st at beg of next row, then at same edge every other row 11 times more, AT THE SAME TIME, when 2 rows have been completed, inc 1 st at side edge on next row, then every other row 3 times more. Work until piece measures 1¾" from beg, end on WS. Do not ch, turn.

Armhole

Sl st across first 3 sts, ch 1, finish row. After all neck dec have been completed, work even on 3 sts until piece measures same length as back. Fasten off.

SLEEVES

Sew shoulder seams. From RS, work 25 sc evenly spaced along armhole edge. Ch 1, turn. Work even in sc until sleeve measures ⅞" from beg. Dec 1 st each side on next row, then every 4th row 5 times more—13 sts. Work even until sleeve measures 3¼" from beg. Fasten off.

FINISHING

Sew side and sleeve seams.

Edging

From RS, join yarn with a sc in side edge of first row of right front, work 59 more sc evenly spaced along entire edge to first row of left front. Ch 1, turn. **Next Row:** Sc in each st across. Do not fasten off.

Right Tie

Tightly crochet a ch to measure 4"-long. Fasten off.

Left Tie

Tightly crochet a ch to measure 4½"-long. Fasten off. Sew left tie to left front. Going from WS to RS, draw left tie through st of first row next to right side seam. To close surplice, tie ties at left side seam.

materials

Yarn
J. & P. Coats Knit-Cro-Sheen Size 10 Crochet Cotton (150y/137m) by Coats & Clark, 1 ball #35 Almond Pink.

Crochet Hook
Size B (1) or size to obtain gauge.

Notions
Tapestry needle.

gauge

16 sc and 18 rows = 2".
FOR PROPER FIT, TAKE THE TIME TO CHECK YOUR GAUGE.

Patriotic Pullovers

These all-American fashions are worn more proudly than ever! The Yankee Doodle polo pullover is crocheted in moss stitch and features single crochet ribbed bands and collar. Three tiny white buttons dot the front.

POLO PULLOVER

Yarn

J. & P. Coats Knit-Cro-Sheen
Size 10 Crochet Cotton
(150y/137m) by Coats & Clark,
1 ball each #126 Spanish Red
(MC) and #1 White (CC).

Crochet Hooks

Steel crochet hook size 4 and
aluminum crochet hook size
B (1) or size to obtain gauge.

Notions

Tapestry needle.
3 white Barbie buttons
#47370 by JHB International.

CROPPED TOP

Yarn

J. & P. Coats Knit-Cro-Sheen
Size 10 Crochet Cotton
(150y/137m) by Coats & Clark,
1 ball each #182 True Blue
(MC) and #126 Spanish Red
(CC).

Crochet Hooks

Steel crochet hook size 4 and
aluminum crochet hook size B
(1) or size to obtain gauge.

Notions

Tapestry needle.
2 white Barbie buttons
#47370 by JHB International.
3 Star Trimmer gold charms
#421 by JHB International.

yankee doodle polo pullover

BACK

Ribbing: Ribbing is made vertically.
With smaller hook and CC, ch 5.
Row 1: Sc in 2nd ch from hook and
in each ch across—4 sts. Ch 1, turn.
Row 2: Working through back lps
only, sc in each st across. Ch 1, turn.
Rep row 2 for rib pat and work even
until piece measures 2¼" from beg.
Ch 1, turn to long edge of ribbing.
Foundation Row (WS): Work 22 sc
evenly spaced across long edge of
ribbing. Change to larger hook. Join
MC, ch 1, turn.
Pattern Stitch
Row 1: * Sc in next st, dc in next st,
rep from * across. Ch 1, turn. Rep
this row for pat st and work even
until piece measures 2¾" from beg.
Fasten off.

FRONT

Work same as for back until piece
measures 2" from beg, end on WS.
Ch 1, turn.
Shape Left Neck
Keeping to pat st, work across first 9
sts, dec 1 st over next 2 sts, ch 1,
turn. Keeping to pat st, dec 1 st at
neck edge every row 4 times more—
6 sts. Fasten off.
Shape Right Neck
From RS, join MC with a sc, then
dec this st with the next st, finish
row. Continue to shape neck same
as for left side.

SLEEVES

Work ribbing same as for back until
piece measures 1⅝" from beg. Ch 1,
turn to long edge of ribbing.
Foundation Row (WS): Work 18 sc
evenly spaced across long edge of
ribbing. Change to larger hook. Join
MC, ch 1, turn. Work even in pat st
same as for back until sleeve measures 1½" from beg. Fasten off.

COLLAR

With smaller hook and CC, ch 7.
Row 1: Sc in 2nd ch from hook and
in each ch across—6 sts. Ch 1, turn.
Row 2: Working through back lps
only, sc in each st across. Ch 1, turn.
Rep row 2 for rib pat and work even
until piece measures 4" from beg.
Fasten off.

FINISHING

Sew shoulder seams. Sew on collar.
Sew on sleeves, centering them at
shoulder seams. Sew side and sleeve
seams. Sew on 3 buttons down
center front, as shown.

POLO PULLOVER

15 sts = 2" (in pat st
using larger hook).

CROPPED TOP

8 sts and 6 rows = 1"
(in hdc using larger hook).
FOR PROPER FIT, TAKE THE
TIME TO CHECK YOUR GAUGE.

Patriotic Pullovers

Accent a simple cropped top with star spangled gold charms to make it extra-special. Make it in half double crochet, then embroider contrasting stripes using running stitches.

The stars 'n stripes make a striking fashion statement. This handsome pullover is made in single crochet and features a modified boat neck, dropped-shoulder sleeves and turned back cuffs.

star spangled cropped top

BACK

Ribbing: Ribbing is made vertically. With smaller hook and MC, ch 5.
Row 1: Sc in 2nd ch from hook and in each ch across—4 sts. Ch 1, turn.
Row 2: Working through back lps only, sc in each st across. Ch 1, turn. Rep row 2 for rib pat and work even until piece measures 2¼" from beg. Ch 1, turn to long edge of ribbing.
Foundation Row (WS): Work 20 sc evenly spaced across long edge of ribbing. Change to larger hook. Ch 2 turn. **Following Row:** Hdc in each st across. Ch 2, turn. Rep this row 7 times more. Fasten off.

FRONT

Work same as for back.

STRAPS

Make 2. With larger hook and MC, ch 20. **Row 1:** Sc in 2nd ch from hook and in each ch across—19 sts. Ch 1, turn. **Row 2:** Sc in each st across. Fasten off.

FINISHING

Sew side seams.
Embroidered Stripes
Using CC, sew running sts (going under and over each hdc st), along rows 2, 4, 6 and 8 on both back and front.
Sew straps to top back edge, positioning them ¾" from side seams. Position each front strap ½" from side seam and secure it in place by sewing a button on top. On front, sew star charms evenly spaced along row 7.

stars 'n stripes pullover

BACK

Ribbing: Ribbing is made vertically. With smaller hook and A, ch 7. **Row 1:** Sc in 2nd ch from hook and in each ch across—6 sts. Ch 1, turn. **Row 2:** Working through back lps only, sc in each st across. Ch 1, turn. Rep row 2 for rib pat and work even until piece measures 3" from beg. Ch 1, turn to long edge of ribbing. **Foundation Row (WS):** Work 31 sc evenly spaced across long edge of ribbing. Change to larger hook. Join B, ch 1, turn.

Stripe Pattern

Row 1: With B, sc in each st across. Ch 1, turn. **Row 2:** With B, sc in each st across. Join A, ch 1, turn. **Row 3:** With A, sc in each st across. Ch 1, turn. **Row 4:** With A, sc in each st across. Join B, ch 1, turn. Rep rows 1-4 for stripe pat and work even until 5 A stripes have been completed, end on WS. Join C, ch 1, turn.

Star Pattern

Rows 1 and 2: Sc in each st across. Ch 1, turn. **Row 3 (RS):** With C, sc in next 3 sts, * with A, sc in next st, with C, sc in next 3 sts, rep from * across. Ch 1, turn. **Row 4:** With C, sc in each st across. Ch 1, turn. **Row 5:** With C, sc in next st, * with A, sc in next st, with C, sc in next 3 sts, rep from * across, end last rep, with C, sc in last st. Ch 1, turn. **Row 6:** Rep row 4. **Row 7:** Rep row 3. **Rows 8 and 9:** Rep row 4. After row 9 is completed, join A, ch 1, turn. Work even for 2 rows, end on RS. Ch 1, turn.

Right Shoulder

Next Row (WS): Work across first 9 sts. Ch 1, turn. Work even for 2 rows. Fasten off.

Left Shoulder

From WS, sk center 13 sts, join A with a sc in next st, work across last 8 sts—9 sts. Work even for 2 rows. Fasten off.

FRONT

Work same as for back.

SLEEVES

Work ribbing same as for back until piece measures 2" from beg. Ch 1, turn to long edge of ribbing.
Foundation Row (WS): Work 25 sc evenly spaced across long edge of ribbing. Change to larger hook. Join B, ch 1, turn. Work stripe pat same as for back and work even until sleeve measures 1½" from beg, end on WS. Inc 1 st each side on next row, then every 6th row twice more—31 sts. Work even until 7 A stripes have been completed. Fasten off.

FINISHING

Sew shoulder seams. Sew on sleeves, centering them at shoulder seams. Sew side and sleeve seams. Turn up cuffs.

STARS 'N STRIPES PULLOVER

Yarn

J. & P. Coats Knit-Cro-Sheen Size 10 Crochet Cotton (150y/137m) by Coats & Clark, 1 ball each #1 White (A), #126 Spanish Red (B) and #87 Dark Royal (C).

Crochet Hooks

Steel crochet hook size 4 and aluminum crochet hook size B (1) or size to obtain gauge.

Notions

Tapestry needle.

notes

1. When changing colors, draw new color through 2 lps on hook to complete sc.
2. When working stripe pattern, carry color not in use loosely along side edge of work.
3. When working star pattern, carry color not in use loosely across WS of work.

gauge

9 sts and 10 rows = 1" (in sc using larger hook). FOR PROPER FIT, TAKE THE TIME TO CHECK YOUR GAUGE.

Flirty Mini

When go-go boots were all the rage, this shift dress was hot! It's short, sleeveless and accented with bold vertical stripes... all the best of 60's couture fashion. Pair it with a hat that's adorned with a long plaited tassel.

Yarn
Pearl Cotton #5 (25m/27.3yd) by DMC, 4 skeins #780 Ultra Very Dk. Topaz (MC) and 1 skein #712 Cream (CC).
Crochet Hook
Size C (2) or size to obtain gauge.
Notions
Tapestry needle.
4 small metal snaps.

dress

FRONT

Made vertically. Beg at side edge, with MC, ch 39. **Row 1:** Sc in 2nd ch from hook and in each ch across—38 sts. Ch 1, turn. **Row 2 (RS):** Working through back lps, sc in each st across. Ch 1, turn. **Row 3:** Working through front lps, sc in each st across. Ch 1, turn. Rep rows 2 and 3 for pat st and work even until piece measures 1⅛" from beg, end on WS. Join CC, ch 1, turn. Work even until piece measures 1⅞" from beg, end on WS. Join MC, ch 1, turn. Work even until piece measures 3" from beg, end on WS. Fasten off.

LEFT BACK

Work same as for front until piece measures 1½" from beg. Fasten off.

RIGHT BACK

Work same as for left back.

FINISHING

Sew a ¾" shoulder seam each side.
Neck Edging
With CC, ch 27. **Row 1:** Sc in 2nd ch from hook and in each ch across—36 sts. Ch 1, turn. Rep row 2 same as for front. Fasten off. Sew edging to neck edge.
Sew side seams leaving ¾" armhole openings. Sew on snaps evenly spaced along back opening.

hat

Made horizontally. Beg at bottom edge, with MC, ch 37. **Row 1:** Sc in 2nd ch from hook and in each ch across—36 sts. Ch 1, turn. **Row 2 (RS):** Working through back lps, sc in each st across. Ch 1, turn. **Row 3:** Working through front lps, sc in each st across. Ch 1, turn. Rep rows 2 and 3 for pat st and work even until piece measures 1¼" from beg, end on WS.
Shape Crown
Dec Row: Working through both lps, * dec 1 st over next 2 sts, rep from * across—18 sts. Fasten off.

FINISHING

Sew back seam. Run a gathering thread around last row. Pull tight to gather; fasten off securely.
Braid
Thread needle with 3 (12"-long) strands of MC. Going from RS to WS, insert needle through center top of hat. Fasten strands securely on WS. On RS of hat, braid strands for 2¼". Knot ends close to end of braid. Trim off excess yarn ¼" from knot.

note

When changing colors, draw new color through 2 lps on hook to complete sc.

gauge

8 sc = 1".
FOR PROPER FIT, TAKE THE TIME TO CHECK YOUR GAUGE.

Night Song Radiance

Barbie® is the shining star in this dazzling strapless evening top with matching neck scarf. Worked in basic single crochet, it's made using royal purple "Artic Rays" yarn. So quick and easy to crochet, you can make it in a wink!

top

Made in one piece. Beg at bottom edge, ch 29. **Row 1:** Sc in 2nd ch from hook and in each ch across—28 sts. Ch 1, turn. **Row 2:** Sc in each st across. Ch 1, turn. Rep row 2 for pat st and work even until piece measures 1¾" from beg. Fasten off.

FINISHING
Sew 3 snaps evenly spaced along back opening, so edges overlap ½".

scarf

Scarf is made vertically. Beg at long side edge, ch 33. **Row 1:** Sc in 2nd ch from hook and in each ch across—32 sts. Ch 1, turn. **Row 2:** Sc in each st across. Ch 1, turn. Rep row 2 for pat st and work even until piece measures ¾" from beg. Fasten off.

materials

Yarn
Artic Rays (8yd/7.3m) by Rainbow Gallery, 2 cards #AR6 Royal Purple.
Crochet Hook
Size D (3) or size to obtain gauge.
Notions
Tapestry needle.
3 small metal snaps.

note

It's sometimes difficult seeing the sts when working with fuzzy yarn. For best results, count sts as you work across each row to make sure you do not skip or miss a st.

gauge

6 sc = 1".
FOR PROPER FIT, TAKE THE TIME TO CHECK YOUR GAUGE.

Picadilly Plaid

pullover

BACK

Beg at bottom edge, with A, ch 23.
Row 1 (RS): Sc in 2nd ch from hook
and in each ch across—22 sts. Ch 1,
turn. **Row 2:** Sc in each st across. Ch
1, turn. Rep row 2 for pat st and
work even until piece measures
1¾" from beg, end on WS. Do
not ch, turn.

Armholes

Sl st across first 2 sts, ch 1, work
across to within last 2 sts—18 sts.
Ch 1, turn. Work even until piece
measures 3⅛" from beg. Fasten off.

FRONT

Work same as for back until piece
measures 2" from beg, end on WS.

Shape Left Neck

Work across first 7 sts, dec 1 st over
next 2 sts—8 sts. Ch 1, turn. Dec 1 st
at same edge every row 4 times
more—4 sts. Work even until piece

measures same length as back to shoulders. Fasten off.

Shape Right Neck
From RS, join A with a sc in next st, AT THE SAME TIME, dec it with next st, finish row—8 sts. Cont to work same as for left side.

SLEEVES
Sew shoulder seams. From RS, work 24 sc evenly spaced along armhole edge. Ch 1, turn. Work even in sc until sleeve measures 1" from beg, end on WS. Dec 1 st each side on next row, then every 4th row 4 times more—14 sts. Work even until sleeve measures 3" from beg, end on WS. Fasten off.

FINISHING
Sew side and sleeve seams.

Neck Ties
On each side of front neck edge, measure and mark ½" down from each shoulder. With A, ch 25, then join yarn with a sc at marker on right front neck edge, work 3 more sc evenly spaced to shoulder. Work 10 sc along back neck edge, then 4 sc evenly spaced along left front neck edge to marker. Ch 26, turn. **Next Row:** Sc in 2nd ch from hook and in each ch and st across. Fasten off. Draw in all loose ends.

skirt

Made in one piece. Beg at bottom edge, with A, ch 50. **Row 1 (WS):** Sc in 2nd ch from hook and in each ch across—49 sts. Join B, ch 1, turn.

Chart
Working in sc (with a ch-1 turn at end of each row), beg chart on **Row 2 (RS)** at W and work to Y. Rep from X to Y twice more, then

end at Z. Work even to Row 28 (RS). Join A, ch 1, turn.

Shape Waist
Dec Row 1 (WS): Sc in first 4 sts, (dec 1 st over next 2 sts, sc in next st, dec 1 st over next 2 sts), [sc in next 3 sts, rep between ( )'s, sc in next st, rep between ( )'s] twice, end sc in next 3 sts, rep between ( )'s, sc in last 4 sts—37 sts. Ch 1, turn. **Following Row:** Sc in each st across. Ch 1, turn. **Dec Row 2:** Sc in first 2 sts, [dec 1 st over next 2 sts, sc in next 2 sts] 8 times, end dec 1 st over next 2 sts, sc in last st—28 sts. Ch 1, turn. **Following Row:** Sc in each st across. Fasten off.

FINISHING
Draw in all loose ends. Sew back seam to within 1" of top edge. Sew snap to waist opening.

Color Key
● Med. Garnet A   ● Black C
□ Lt. Drab Brown B   ○ Cream D

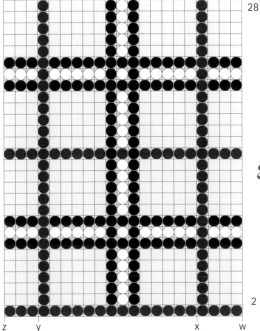

materials

Yarn
Pearl Cotton #5 (25m/27.3yd) by DMC, 4 skeins #815 Med. Garnet (A), 2 skeins #613 Very Lt. Drab Brown (B), and 1 skein each #310 Black (C) and #712 Cream (D).

Crochet Hook
Size B (1) or size to obtain gauge.

Notions
Tapestry needle.
1 small metal snap.

notes

1. When changing colors, draw new color through 2 lps on hook to complete sc.
2. Only color B gets carried loosely across WS of work.
3. Use a separate 36"-long strand of color for each vertical stripe on skirt.
4. Do not carry colors along side edge of work, instead, cut and join colors as needed.

gauge

17 sc and 22 rows = 2".
FOR PROPER FIT, TAKE THE TIME TO CHECK YOUR GAUGE.

Budding Beauty

Silver has never sparkled so beautifully! This simple, single crochet metallic tube-style dress is topped with a soft pink angora off-the-shoulder collar that's accented with a sweet ribbon rose.

dress

Made vertically in one piece. Beg at back side edge, with smaller hook and A, ch 41. **Row 1:** Sc in 2nd ch from hook and in each ch across—40 sts. Ch 1, turn. **Row 2:** Working through back lps only, sc in each st across. Ch 1, turn. Rep row 2 for pat st and work even until piece measures 5¼" from beg. Fasten off.

COLLAR

Beg at bottom edge, with larger hook and B, ch 42. **Row 1:** Sc in 2nd ch from hook and in each ch across—41 sts. Ch 1, turn. **Row 2:** Working through back lps only, sc in each st across. Ch 1, turn. Rep row 2 for pat st and work even until piece measures ¾" from beg. Fasten off.

belt

Beg at bottom edge, with smaller hook and A, ch 28. **Row 1:** Sc in 2nd ch from hook and in each ch across—27 sts. Ch 1, turn. **Row 2:** Working through back lps only, sc in each st across. Ch 1, turn. Rep row 2 for pat st and work even until piece measures ½" from beg. Fasten off.

FINISHING

Sew back seam on dress. Sew 1 snap to collar so ends of collar overlap ⅜". Sew 1 ribbon rose to center front of collar and 1 to center back. Tack center bottom edge of collar to top center front edge of dress. Sew rem snap to belt so that ends of belt overlap ⅜".

Yarn
A Taste of Glitz
(25g/190yd) by K1C2,
1 cone #120 Pink
Champagne (A) and
Rainbow Angora
(7yd/6.4m) by Rainbow
Gallery, 1 card #RA11 Baby
Pink (B).

Crochet Hooks
Size C (2) and D (3) or
sizes to obtain gauges.

Notions
Tapestry needle.
2 small metal snaps.
2 small Sheer Ribbon
Roses #168 Colonial Rose
by Offray.

gauges

8 sc = 1" (using A and
smaller hook).
5 sc = 1" (using B and
larger hook).
FOR PROPER FIT, TAKE THE
TIME TO CHECK YOUR
GAUGES.

Abbreviations

approx approximately

beg begin(ning)

CC contrasting color

ch chain(s)

cont continu(e)(ing)

dc double crochet

dec decrease(ing) (see glossary)

g gram(s)

hdc half double crochet

inc increas(e)(ing) (see glossary)

lp(s) loop(s)

m meter(s)

mm millimeter(s)

MC main color

oz ounce(s)

pat(s) pattern(s)

rem remain(s)(ing)

rep repeat

rnd(s) round(s)

RS right side(s)

sc single crochet

sk skip

sl slip

sl st slip st

st(s) stitch(es)

tog together

WS wrong side(s)

yd yard(s)

yo yarn over

* = repeat directions following * as many times as indicated.

[ ] = repeat directions inside brackets as many times as indicated.

( ) = work directions contained inside parentheses in st indicated.

GLOSSARY

decrease 1 dc [Yo. Insert hook into next st and draw up a lp. Yo and draw through 2 lps] twice, yo and draw through all 3 lps on hook.

decrease 1 hdc [Yo, insert hook into next st and draw up a lp] twice, yo and draw through all 5 lps on hook.

decrease 1 sc [Insert hook into next st and draw up a lp] twice, yo and draw through all 3 lps on hook.

increase 1 stitch Work 2 sts in 1 st.

join yarn with a dc Make a lp and slip onto hook, then yo. Insert hook into st. Yo and draw up a lp. [Yo and draw through 2 lps on hook] twice.

join yarn with a hdc Make a lp and slip onto hook, then yo. Insert hook into st. Yo and draw up a lp. Yo and draw through 3 lps on hook.

join yarn with a sc Make a lp and slip onto hook. Insert hook into st. Yo and draw up a lp. Yo and draw through 2 lps on hook.

work even Continue in pattern without increasing or decreasing.

Helpful Hints

Included here is a basic schematic for a hand crocheted sweater for your Barbie® doll. My suggested hook sizes are steel hooks size 8 and 4 and aluminum hook sizes B, C and D. The corresponding yarns that work best are crochet cottons, and fingering- and sport-weight yarns. Larger hooks and heavier yarns can look big and unflattering on your doll. I've used a wide range of fine yarns including: cottons, wool, acrylics, angora, novelty blends and even cashmere. Crochet for Barbie® is a great way to use up leftover yarns. If you don't use the yarns suggested, be sure to get the same gauge given for each piece.

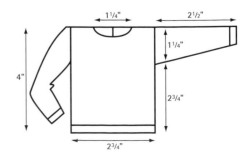

RESOURCES

Coats & Clark
Attn. Consumer Service
PO Box 12229
Greenville, SC 29612-0229

DMC Corporation
Port Kearny Bldg. 10A
South Kearny, NJ 07032-4688

Froehlich Wolle
Distributed by
WheelSmith Wools
PO Box 388
Centrehall, PA 16828
(877) 474-0026

JCA, Inc.
35 Scales Lane
Townsend, MA 01469-1094

K1C2, LLC
2220 Eastman Ave. #105
Ventura, CA 93003

Lion Brand Yarn Co.
34 West 15th Street
New York, New York 10011
www.lionbrand.com

ME Enterprises
Available from
Sunshine Crafts
PO Box 301
Largo, FL 33779-0301
(800) 729-2878
www.sunshinecrafts.com

Prism
2995 30th Avenue North
St. Petersburg, FL 33713-2925
(727) 327-3100

Rainbow Gallery
7412 Fulton Ave.
N. Hollywood, CA 91605
www.rainbowgallery.com

Rowan Yarns
5 Northern Blvd.
Amherst, NH 03031

Big Eye Needle and Flexible Magnetic Needle
Available from
Fire Mountain Gems
#1 Fire Mountain Way
Grants Pass, OR 97526-2373
(800) 355-2137
www.firemountaingems.com

JHB Buttons
(800) 525-9007

Mill Hill
Gay Bowles Sales, Inc.
PO Box 1060
Janesville, WI 53547-1060
(608) 754-9466
www.millhill.com

C.M. Offray & Son, Inc.
Chester, NJ 07930-0601
(908) 879-4700

Contact the companies listed for yarn purchasing and mail-order information. Resource information is current at time of publication.

Acknowledgements

I would like to thank...

the staff of SOHO Publishing, including Trisha Malcolm, Carla Scott, Chi Ling Moy, Lisa Ventry, Christina Batch, Rebecca Rosen, Veronica Manno and Theresa McKeon for their personal and professional support, and to photographers Bobb Connors and Jack Deutsch and Associates for the great pictures and long hours. Special thanks to Joe and John DeGorter for dependable transportation.

Thanks to all my friends and family who encouraged me and endured with good humor my apartment filled with yarn and dozens of Barbie® and Ken® dolls. Especially Anne Rose and Emily Brenner, Chris Kitch, David Farrow and Vita and Vincent Caputo.

Kisses to my husband Howard and sons Scott, Jeff, and Ken who remain my most loyal, loving fans.

My gratitude to Mattel for allowing me to continue to create for Barbie® and her fans.

Most of all, a multitude of thanks to Pat Harste for her invaluable contributions to this book. Her crocheting skills, editorial eye, ability to communicate easy-to-follow instructions, impeccable good taste and unfailing good humor made this project a joy for me to complete. Thanks, also, to Emily Harste and the Harste household.

None of this could be possible without the enduring popularity of Barbara Millicent Roberts. She's a real doll!